MW01166356

DEAR MARIAN MOVEMENT

Let God be God

By: William A. Reck

Published by:
The Riehle Foundation
P.O. Box 7
Milford, OH 45150

The author and publisher herein recognize and accept that the final authority regarding all private revelation rests with the Holy See of Rome to whose judgment we willingly submit.

Published in the USA by: The Riehle Foundation
P.O. Box 7
Milford, OH 45150

Individuals seeking additional copies of this book should contact The Riehle Foundation.

Bookstores and book distributors seeking additional copies should contact:
Faith Publishing Company
P.O. Box 237
Milford, OH 45150

Library of Congress Catalog #96-68951

ISBN # 1-877678-42-2

TABLE OF CONTENTS

Introduction

Dear Reader:

I have to assume you are reading this book because you have some special interest in the realm of private revelation—apparitions, visions, supernatural manifestations and the like. Most of this activity currently involves the Blessed Virgin Mary. As such, in this book it is referred to as the "Marian Movement."

Your interest may be positive or negative. You may be reading this because of your great support and involvement with current claimed apparitions, or because you have also experienced something special: a rosary turned color, solar phenomena, an unexplainable photograph or maybe just the sudden scent of roses. Perhaps you are aware of a healing or some prophecy that touched your life. It's becoming rather difficult to not be affected by private revelation in some way or another today. It's everywhere—even on national TV.

On the other hand, you may be reading this because all of this claimed miracle and apparition business has you concerned, or has had a negative influence on you. You may feel it is out of control, or now involves many people whose good intentions and imaginations have run away with them. You may believe some need professional medical help, or perhaps that the wrong spirit is leading many people astray.

I am inclined to believe that all of the above situations and attitudes are accurate, and very realistic.

v

In my case, I am firmly entrenched right in the middle of both positions. In 1986 my career (as well as Fran's, my late wife) was chucked aside and The Riehle Foundation became our life. Since the Foundation is dedicated to The Blessed Virgin Mary and her role in our salvation, much of what we do involves her in one way or another. My personal "conversion" in my spiritual life came from a pilgrimage to Fatima and Medjugorje in 1986. I have seen the "signs and wonders." I have been touched by the Gospa. I believe I was called by the Gospa. Through the Foundation, I have been involved in the publishing and distribution of over 6,000,000 books, brochures and newsletters that mostly had Mary as a theme. I do not know how many rosaries, scapulars, medals and prayer cards we have distributed. I continue to try to dedicate my time and efforts to the Mother of Jesus (usually aware that I could be doing a far better job of it), so, make no mistake about it, my support of and my devotion to this Lady is strong indeed. Maybe even far more than that of many others.

I also now see myself on the fringe of the second classification listed above—the group that sees a negative image to some of this—and it is in this vein that this book is written. Whether you support all of this private revelation and supernatural phenomena, or can find no reason to accept it, one thing is now certain:

> It is largely flying out of control, and often without a pilot. And when there is a pilot, it may be the one you don't want.

In just the last six years, hundreds of claimed seers and locutionists have come on the scene. Hundreds of new "message books" and tapes have made their appearance as well. Speaking tours for visionaries and the production of sensational new revelations became a whole new industry. Humility and obedience to the Church have not always been a part of it. Still, many good things happened. Much of it is very hard to dispute. People's lives were touched and they responded—and responded, and responded.

In this euphoria produced by Jesus and His Mother apparently coming to directly speak to their people, the criticism of visionaries has seemed to become the forbidden fruit. We now seem to find no problem at all in identifying and promoting visionaries and messengers, and all too eagerly seem to snap up their words of wisdom and prophecies. But a pax on you and your family if you dare speak negatively of any or refuse to listen to Jesus or His Mother through some "voicebox."

What all of this really comes down to is the simple fact that I personally believe it is not always Jesus or His Mother that you are listening to in the first place. There is a need to accept at least the possibility that much of this supernatural phenomena is not authentic. This process is known as discernment, and that is what this book is all about.

In this process of discernment put into printed form, one invariably winds up identifying a certain apparition site or visionary that one does not believe in, whether by name or not. Well, we are probably at the point where the facts need to come out, but you also need to be aware that there is no condemnation intended, no planned slander, no seal of approval or stamp of rejection. You are free to believe or not believe as you see fit. Not even the Magisterium of the Church suggests you must or should believe in private revelation. But she does rule against those that she feels can and will harm your faith.

So then who am I to say. I cannot in anyway prove that any claimed visionary does or does not have visions. Neither can you. Neither can anybody else. So there is no intent here to even try to prove the impossible. We can verify events, statements and the like, or prove such and such didn't happen, or was wrong. But we cannot prove anyone does or does not have locutions or visions.

In the past fifteen to twenty years, complaints of the laity as to watered-down Catholicism have been common. And with good reason, probably. Much confusion and dissension exists in the Church. That fact, coupled with the elimination of certain restrictions of the Church dealing with private revelations, and the advancements of mass communication, have induced the faithful to "go where the action is," and where it is, more often than not, is at apparition sites. The enthusiasm all of this provoked is undeniable. And it certainly has provided some good fruits as well. What is now apparent, however, is that **discernment** is not a popular word in the private revelation business. Included in the definitions of that word is the understanding that "judging" is indeed part of the process. It leaves us, then, with a preliminary discernment need regarding Christ's admonition: *Judge not, lest you be judged* (*Matt.* 7:1). This is already getting difficult.

One key ingredient in the discernment process seems to be the recognition that some of this private revelation could be the work of Satan. That seems to be something many of us just don't want to accept. We're too caught up in all this "good fruits" and inspired words. How could this be wrong?

Unfortunately, the answer to that question is often a simple, "It can't possibly be wrong," statement, and so it is accepted as right. No further questions need to be asked. No further discernment is needed, apparently.

This book is based on the fact that we **do** need to ask. We need to find out answers to any areas of concern we have regarding any private revelation from any claimed messenger, anywhere. We have both a right and a responsibility to question. If that is judging, then so be it. It is also part of discernment.

You do **not** have to believe any visionary. And if you don't, that is not slander; nor is it falsely accusing someone. Your difference of opinion is not a personal attack on another, even if the claimed "another" is the Blessed Virgin Mary or Jesus. The proof of that claimed message is always on the messenger, not on you.

The other side of this coin, of course, is that apparitions are real. They are as old as the Bible, as old as our first parents. And there is plenty of documentation and positive fruits available concerning claimed apparitions of today to be quite sure that something very powerful is indeed taking place.

The need is for some strong guidelines to separate the wheat from the chaff. Or at least the effort to make sure we are following only the right spirit. That is what this book is about and there is a need to identify situations to use as examples: not to try to label them as bad examples, but to show areas where there is a need for you to question, and why.

CHAPTER 1

Why Devotion to Mary?

"And whom do you say that I am?" Jesus asked His apostles.

Today, the same question might apply more to the Blessed Virgin Mary. In our world, angels, and certainly the Blessed Virgin Mary are very hot items. Visions are everywhere (and corresponding $$$). Heavenly messages seem to abound. Is this something new? Is the world about to come apart? How does all of this fit in with the accepted Word of God in the Bible? And how does the Blessed Virgin Mary fit into it?

During the years of 1987 to 1990 in particular, my late wife (Fran) and I gave many presentations on the claimed apparitions of Mary in Medjugorje, in what was then Yugoslavia. Having experienced some rather startling episodes there, along with a rather profound conversion, I felt I had some knowledge on the subject.

It was sometime in 1989, I believe, and I was to give a presentation at a parish to a **Legion of Mary** group. It was a rather small group, but most striking about the gathering was the fact that most of them would qualify for senior citizen discounts (so do I). I sat through and participated in a part of their meeting and prayer session. It sparked a certain interest in me. The Legion of Mary, after all, seems to have been labeled as one of those "pre-Vatican II," old-fashioned, dying sodalities now just composed of older women. A look

1

at the history of that organization provided a most interesting paradox. It is an excellent analysis, and at the same time a comparison of where Marian devotion is today, where it came from, and just who Mary is.

Before we take a closer look at this organization, there is a need to first define what is meant by the "**Marian Movement**," since that term will be used often in this book. The term "Marian Movement" is not to be confused with an organization, international in scope, known as "The Marian Movement of Priests." Here we are speaking of the overall, general devotion to the Blessed Virgin Mary as practiced by individuals and organizations, laity, clergy and religious. It is the piety and recognition given to Mary as the Mother of Our Lord and Savior, but not a formal organization nor title of some existing, professional apostolate. It is simply the interest of many millions of people who see the Blessed Virgin Mary in some special capacity.

And guess what! That's been around as long as Pentecost. And the Legion of Mary is simply part of that movement.

The Legion of Mary began very inauspiciously in Dublin, Ireland, in September of 1921. A group of zealous and devoted women, auxiliaries of the St. Vincent de Paul Society there, wanted to form an organization and ministry of their own. They were encouraged and led by a young St. Vincent de Paul member named Frank Duff, and the Legion was born. It was first and foremost a program of personal sanctification for its members, and then an apostolic activity, in the name of Our Lady, dedicated to evangelization on behalf of the Church. A weekly spiritual meeting was at the center and from that they started to visit jails, hospitals and ghettos. They established night shelters for the homeless and unemployed. Catholic literature was produced and distributed widely. The fallen were being brought back to Mass, spiritual renewal was evident, and conversions prospered. Through it all, prayer was always at the forefront, and dedication to the Mother of God, the foundation for their activities. They, like Mary, worked to lead people to Jesus.

The Legion rapidly spread throughout Europe, and then the whole world. It has been personally endorsed by Popes ever since its humble beginnings. The success of its com-

mitment in the name of Mary and the conversions it produced, also brought anticipated response from a world
growing more and more pagan as the twentieth century
lurched forward into secular humanism and Communism.
The Legion was especially hated in the Soviet Union for
example, as well as in China, where they performed yeoman
work in preparing Catholics for the takeover of the Communist Chinese. As is the case with all Missionaries for Christ,
the Legion was not without its persecuted, and martyred, as
Communism rolled over two-thirds of the earth just as was
predicted by the Blessed Virgin Mary at a little village
named **Fatima**, in Portugal, in 1917.

The great success the Legion of Mary achieved was evidently not the result of just the personalities of its members.
It obviously stemmed from the foundation built by Duff and
that group of ladies in Dublin in 1921. Their charter became
their hallmark of success . . . that and the complete childlike
trust in the Blessed Virgin. Suddenly, by the middle of this
century, there were literally thousands and thousands of
chapters of the Legion and many hundreds of thousands of
active members . . . and growing still more.

The foundation of that success? At least in part, it
stemmed from the fact that the Legion of Mary operated
through a parish, and as part of a parish. It became a viable
group within a parish and under control thereof. The official Legion Handbook for members contains 285 pages. It is
heavenly structured. That handbook spells out in detail that
the Legion was established to operate under ecclesiastical
guidance and that every chapter is at the disposal of the
bishop of the diocese and of the parish priest. It is interesting that Pope John XXIII, who some claim was responsible
for the demotion of the Blessed Virgin Mary in the scheme
of things, stated: "The Legion of Mary presents the true face
of the Catholic Church."

So what happened to it then? A real good question. The
Legion of Mary along with a number of other Marian organizations . . . that Marian Movement we identified . . .
seemed to dissolve. By the time we got to the 1980s, it was
quickly becoming just a collection of loose-knit apparitions
and visionaries pushing a whole new Marian piety, often
without any direction at all.

The goal here is to try and find out just what did happen. What is the role of the Blessed Virgin Mary in the Church today? Where did all that former Marian devotion go? And what about all of these claimed new apparitions and messages being received today (supposedly) by so many seers across the country proclaiming imminent disaster? Are they all for real? And how does one discern it all?

I should state here that I do not believe in probably 75% of the claimed visionaries and alleged messengers running around today. But it also needs to be stated that in 1986, I completely chucked my career because of an apparition (as did Fran), and the two of us committed the rest of our lives to the ministry of Our Lady through The Riehle Foundation, without a whole lot of thought or concern as to materialistic security. The results . . . our growth and success . . . have been a little staggering. As such, I do not believe I have to defend my allegiance to the Mother of God, or to His Church. I pledge support to the Pope, the Magisterium, and dedication to the **Two Hearts**. So, any negative views expressed in this book are not personal rejections of individuals, seers, apparition sites, message books, etc., but simply true and real concern for the Marian Movement which is so under attack today, and which I believe is showing signs of coming apart at the seams. It must be preserved.

Toward that point of view, a question is posed here to the reader:

Where do you think the Church would be today without the Marian Movement, or without Pope John Paul II?

Please give that a moment's thought here. We will try to answer that question later in this book—a question I believe is vitally important to our time, and to the Church.

But before we get into all of the apparition debate, it might help immensely if we can cover a little Marian history and define just what the Church's position is—or is not—regarding this little mentioned lady of the Bible, this Virgin who became the Mother of our Lord and Savior, and who evidently plays such an important role in our lives and our eternal salvation, and who is also our Mother, the new Eve. On a personal note, I might add that she is even more important than that to me. She is my buddy, my prayer partner; she to whom Fran formally consecrated her life; she who has manifested her presence to me in special ways a hundred times over the past ten years; she who keeps bringing me closer and closer to her Son; she whom I love.

So who is this woman? Who is the modest and humble Virgin of obedience, always in the background, and where did all this "Marian devotion" come from? And just how current is it?

Fortunately, there are literally hundreds and hundreds of books available to you that address those issues, so we don't need to try and cover it all here. Just a little history review should do.

Mary in Church History

This devotion called the Marian Movement? And apparitions and visions? Is this all a johnny-come-lately event, a false piety that is simply the product of a guilt-ridden society?

Well not hardly. Apparitions are forever; and devotion to Mary goes all the way back to the beginning of the Church itself.

It is interesting that many Protestant denominations are stuck on the concept that Marian devotion is the result of a Church gone bad, somewhere after the fourth or fifth century, and that this all got straightened out when Martin Luther did his thing giving birth to the Protestant Reformation. History shows that Catholic beliefs, including devotion to the Blessed Virgin Mary, have been constant all the way back to the first century of the Church, and that Martin Luther and John Calvin also had a strong devotion to Mary. Apparently it was evident even to the very early Church that Mary was to play a significant role in the spread of the faith and the salvation of mankind.

Though little is provided us in the Bible regarding Mary's life, it is rather amazing how quickly her role was recognized by the early Church, and how many connections were made concerning her role, to the available Scriptures of the

Old Testament. For example, there are extensive accounts of how Mary fits the role of "The New Eve" and the "New Ark of the Covenant." The initial defense of these titles being given to Mary goes all the way back to St. Polycarp, Justin Martyr, and Irenaeus. Irenaeus, the most important theologian of the second century, and martyred for his beliefs in the year 202, developed the Mary-Eve antithesis in the face of the heretical Gnostics.

St. Jerome is generally recognized—by all Christians—as the "Father of Biblical Science." It was Jerome who gave the world the **Vulgate**, the pivotal foundation for all future Bible translations. It was also Jerome (342-420) who defended the virginity of Mary in those first few centuries of the Church. In the same era, Mary's role was defined in the writings of St. Athanasius, St. Ambrose and St. Augustine. By the year 431 A.D., belief in the perpetual virginity of Mary was well founded and proclaimed, and in that same year, the *Council of Ephesus* declared her the "Mother of God."

The *Second Vatican Council*, repeating a phrase from Pope Pius IX, confirmed this belief stating: "The Blessed Virgin was eternally predestined, in conjunction with the Incarnation of the Divine Word, to be the Mother of God." It's all a confirmation of the Gospel of St. Luke who witnesses to the belief of the primitive Church by giving us the words of Mary's *Magnificat*:

> *"All ages to come will call me blessed ... God who is mighty has done great things for me"* (*Lk.* 1:48).

After the Council of Ephesus, there followed the construction of some of the great cathedrals of the world, erected in honor of the Mother of Our Lord (St. Mary Major for example). As early as the fifth century, Christians were celebrating a "memorial of Mary," prayer in recognition of her death, and by the sixth century, homilies on her "Assumption" appear. Throughout the writings of the early Church devotion to Mary is constant following her death. The term "Mediatrix" is not just something coined in this century:

> "Since early times, but especially after the Council of Ephesus, devotion to Mary in the Church

has grown wondrously. The People of God through the ages have shown her veneration and love. They have called upon her in prayer and they imitate her. All these ways of praising Mary draw us closer to Christ, for when Mary is honored, her Son is duly acknowledged, loved and glorified, and His Commandments are observed."

So stated the document of Vatican II, *Dogmatic Constitution on the Church*.

That early devotion, as confirmed by the Council, developed into specific feast days, aspects of the liturgy, and a growing number of sacramentals and prayer rituals. Intercession through Mary was definitely in. So were apparitions of her.

The Rosary, generally believed to have been revealed to St. Dominic in the early 13th century by Our Lady, may even go back much farther than that. One account has it that it dates back to the laity attempting to participate in the Monks daily chanting of the 150 Psalms at the monastery. It was stated that the 150 Psalms became 150 *Our Fathers*, then a psalter of 150 praises of Mary, and finally, the Rosary. Regardless of the time frame involved, the apparent apparition of Mary to Dominic was confirmed many times over during the next six centuries through appearances of Mary to many, always with the call for prayer and conversion . . . and to pray the Rosary. There is not time or space here to list all of the Popes who have endorsed the Rosary. The list is long and their pronouncements strong. Interestingly, one is Pope John XXIII. Many claim that in his name, and through *Vatican Council II*, they have been authorized to ignore the Rosary . . . or even Mary. In *Journal of a Soul* he tells us that from 1953 until his death, he himself recited all fifteen decades every day.

In the year 1251, through a reported apparition of Mary to Simon Stock, Prior General of a Carmelite Order, the Brown Scapular of Our Lady of Mount Carmel came into being. Many special privileges are associated with this scapular, and many miracles attributed to it, as is the case with the Rosary. These graces, or privileges, became known as the

"Sabbatine Privilege," announced through a special document by Pope John XXII, March 3, 1322.

Documented miracles connected with the Rosary are even more numerous, and astounding. Fr. Albert Shamon, in his book *The Power of the Rosary*, gives an excellent account of many of them. They are prominent events in world history and undeniable as to their existence.

Detailed accounts of appearances by Mary, and by Our Lord and Savior, became more and more numerous and started to touch the lives of people around the world. Perhaps we all need to take a closer look at the history of our faith and spend a little more time trying to figure out just how all of this information reached so many people in so many corners of the world—and none of them with a computer, a telephone, a printing press, a TV, or a fax machine. Do you suppose God is actually powerful enough to reach the whole world just by His own merit? How totally helpless we are in our pride.

At any rate, by the time the world had turned its back on its Mother in the Middle Ages (The Protestant Reformation, the Age of Reason, etc.), Mary had become an integral part of our Christian faith. Since the first and second centuries when St. Polycarp, Justin Martyr, and Irenaeus were offering their lives for the Blessed Virgin Mary and the faith of the Church of her Son, Jesus the Christ, up to this present age, no single figure in the history of the world, save for Jesus, has had more coverage than Mary. Cathedrals, Churches, sacramentals and chaplets of all kinds, paintings, sculptures, icons, hymns, endless books and works of art, even cities, towns, rivers, and mountains, all have been created, produced or named in her honor.

There are now so many scapulars and medals attributed to Mary that you are hard pressed to ever get them all around your neck, not to mention the mountain of holy cards and prayer cards produced in her honor. Of prime importance became the emerging devotion to her "Immaculate Heart" and the "Most Sacred Heart of Jesus." And the Rosary has become so important that it is the only prayer form that has its own feast day, October 7th. This concept appears to be in the midst of change, however, in keeping with the importance of the Two Hearts as mentioned above.

The *Chaplet of Divine Mercy*, offered in behalf of the Sacred Heart of Jesus, has become very popular (as well as very important), and the first Sunday after Easter has already been established as **Divine Mercy Sunday**.

And, of course, there is need to give a few lines to recognize that a new world was discovered and that this same Lady played a most important part in that event to. She still does, and in fact, that final climax of her importance to the world and to this country is yet to be written. Perhaps it is being written now.

Mary's presence is stamped all over the developmental process of America. The country was discovered on a ship bearing her name, and the entire country eventually became formally dedicated to her. In 1531 her growing appearances to the world reached the American continent with her apparitions in Guadalupe to Juan Diego. It would hardly seem mere coincidence that this country which became the most profitable, powerful, free, and advanced society in the world, is also the country known as Our Lady's land.

In a predominantly non-Catholic country, her name is one of the most common given to newborn girls and over 60 cities and towns bear her name as well. So do scores of cathedrals, and thousands of parishes are dedicated to her. Hundreds of high schools, colleges, and religious orders are named for her. The growth of this country mirrored the devotion offered to the Blessed Virgin Mary. The tragedy of what eventually happened to this success story we shall cover shortly.

In Europe, devotion to the Blessed Virgin was becoming formalized and the printing press was providing for the distribution of extensive works dedicated to Our Lady. Foremost among these authors were Alphonsus Mary de Liguori and Louis Mary de Montfort. Mary had become extremely prominent, if not famous. She was seen at LaSalette, and at Lourdes. The Miraculous Medal was making its appearance and the dogma of the "Immaculate Conception" was on the threshold.

Shortly the world would be near destroying itself with the arrival of the twentieth century. She would be there again to advise . . . at Fatima.

Skipping ahead to our present era it seems not too much has changed. Mankind still stumbles about, unable or unwilling to unite with each other or recognize the truths of the requests of its Creator. And while we can admit to the fact that we have not achieved the conversion Our Lord asked of us many centuries ago, we also haven't been able to unite our effects as to Mary's role either.

In the American Catholic Bishops Pastoral of 1973, *Behold Your Mother*, the Conference of Bishops stated:

"For too long Mary's place in Catholic doctrine and even more in Catholic devotion has been a sharp point of difference with other Christians of the West. What began in the Reformation as a reaction against certain abuses, soon led in some quarters to forbidding all invocation of the saints, even of Mary, and to a diminished sense of the communion of saints. Throughout the Reformation and Counter-Reformation, excesses abounded on both sides. Protestant polemicists made a battle cry of the supposedly fatal choices: Christ or Mary, Scripture or Tradition, grace or freedom, God or man, as if Catholics did not also accept Christ and the Bible and the supremacy of grace and God as central to the faith.

"The Catholic counterattack exalted and extolled Mary as 'conqueror of all heresy.' It seemed to many Protestants that the Roman Catholic Church had moved even farther away from Christ, the Center, when Pius IX defined the Immaculate Conception of Mary in 1854, and Pius XII her Assumption in 1950 . . . Another difficulty among Christians is the relationship between Scripture, Tradition and the Church's teaching role. How have Catholics come to regard as revealed truth such doctrines as Mary's Immaculate Conception and Assumption, in the absence of clear Biblical evidence?"

Study of the Bishops Pastoral is recommended for it is a most excellent and informative document. Regardless, defining the above points of difference have still not been resolved . . . and perhaps never will be. But as we head into a new century, and to many, into the "end times," apparitions and visions might prove to play a major role in the outcome, either for or against the unity sought, and the acceptance of Mary's role.

It is, perhaps, a time where we suddenly feel the need to control the supernatural instead of simply letting God be God.

CHAPTER 2

Doctrines and Devotions

The growth of the Marian Movement in the Church was largely dependent upon the doctrines and devotions that had also developed. That would come as no surprise. What might be somewhat surprising is that in both cases apparitions and visions of Mary apparently played a major role. The same could be said for various devotions pertaining to Jesus, such as devotion to His Most Sacred Heart. Special feast days, liturgies, litanies, novenas, and sacramentals can be tied to these appearances. The end result is that over the past several centuries Popes have responded in what is almost complete unison as to the role of Mary in our lives and in the Church. A number of Mary's titles can be traced back to a specific appearance where she supposedly came to a seer under that title. Some were a factor in Marian dogmas proclaimed by the Church following an apparition.

And such may be the case now where there is a movement underway to have Mary proclaimed as "Coredemptrix, Mediatrix, and Advocate." The movement is being sponsored by the laity in form of petition to the Holy See to have such a dogma enacted. While it is a definition of a role Mary obviously plays in our lives, the promotion of this dogma may have become confused . . . not so much as to just words comprising a title, but in the form and fashion some are promoting it. We will come back to that topic.

In defense of such a proposed dogma, one might want to study a booklet authored by Francis Ripley, and published by **Tan Books & Publishers, Inc.**, Rockford, Illinois in 1973. The book is titled *Mary, Mother of the Church.* It would be a good reference book for those who are proposing the above referenced and desired dogma. This booklet of 85 pages contains hundreds of specific quotations regarding the Blessed Virgin Mary in the form of her titles, her role, her powers, devotions and honors accorded her, and the position of the Church regarding this most special lady. The quotations come from dozens of Popes in Allocutions, Apostolic Letters, and Encyclicals, as well as from exhortations given in various addresses. Additional quotations come from some of the more pronounced letters or books provided by these leaders of the Church over the years. Common among these various titles and honors given to Mary are the words "Mediatrix," "Advocate," "Auxiliatrix," and "Helper" (or intercessor).

So complete and profound is this list of exhortations to Mary that it is impossible to simply try and pick out a few to show here. Suffice it to say that everything we might want to examine regarding Mary's role is included, especially from the notable Marian Popes: Pope Leo XIII, Benedict XV, Pius X, Pius XII, and Paul VI. In our own day, Pope John Paul II will most surely go down in history as a great and Marian Pope. To her, his pontificate was dedicated: *"Totus, Tuus."* It was John Paul II who instigated only the second Marian Year in the history of the Church in 1987.

Much of this honor afforded Mary through the teachings of Church leaders, and supported by the faithful, seems to have been built around various appearances of Mary, particularly in the 1800s. But it was the events in Fatima, Portugal, in 1917, that truly gave rise to apparitions and visions, and especially to the Marian Movement.

Fatima, it appears, brought a new dimension to Marian devotion and to the concept of apparitions. Whether it was all for the better remains to be seen, but at least on the surface it was. The age of apparitions was here, and many, I believe, also thought the "Age of Mary" was here as well (many believe that age is just now coming into being).

Regardless, it becomes almost absurd to dispute some of the incredible events which took place at Fatima. They are all a part of history, and easily verified. To begin with, it was the first time a specific miracle was predicted giving the exact date, place and time it would take place, and the invitation to bring every unbeliever in the world to witness it. And, it happened. The prophecies at Fatima concerning the future of the world, particularly Russia, were astounding. And, they also became reality. Marian devotion was to hit an all time high, especially in the United States.

In the early 20th century the Catholic Church was thriving in the United States, and the American Bishops were solidly entrenched in the Marian Movement (can you imagine). A mammoth shrine, the National Shrine of the Immaculate Conception, one of the ten great basilicas of the world was to be erected in Washington, D.C. **The Legion of Mary** and the **Sodality of Our Lady** were working through over 14,000 chapters. An additional apostolate, **Catholic Action**, brought thousands of additional Catholics into the Marian Movement each year. Books and magazines involving Mary flourished, and an incredible gentleman, by the name of John Haffert, started an apostolate at the end of World War II known as **The Blue Army.** It would quickly generate a membership that totaled in the millions and spread worldwide. Fatima became the world's pilgrimage site and the center of conversions. The success of the Blue Army is unprecedented and by 1960, in the middle of the "cold War," while openly despised by Communist governments, the apostolate had established an international center and convention facility at Fatima.

The Legion of Mary and **The Militia of the Immaculata** (Maximilian Kolbe) were prospering and the Legion of Mary was particularly successful in promoting the faith through devotion to Mary, by and through participation within the parishes. The Legion was also particularly effective, combined with the Blue Army, in providing a strong example to students in Catholic schools. There weren't many children in those schools who did not know about the Rosary, or how to say one. Compare that with today.

Father Peyton and the use of the radio, ("Family Rosary") came along supporting Marian devotion in parishes across the country including First Saturday devotions, litanies and Rosary prayer groups. To add to the impetus, 1954 was declared a "Marian Year" by the Vatican. I believe Church records will substantiate the fact that in the decade of the fifties, and up to Vatican Council II, vocations showed great growth and Church attendance was at an all-time high.

And suddenly, it was gone. Whatever happened to that wonderful quote from the United States Bishops that we read earlier in this book, about how they decried the lost devotion to Mary?

The weakening of the Church in the United States after the Second Vatican Council apparently began with the sexual revolution of the sixties. Again, I believe Church records will show that almost all of our current confusion and dissent from Papal teaching today relates to sexuality (contraception, divorce, abortion, homosexuality, celibacy, ordination of women, premarital sex, acceptance of pornography, etc.). The encyclical, *Humane Vitae* seemed to be the catalyst. Those same Church records will support the fact that Mary was right in the middle of it all—whether we knew it or not. As dissent increased in the Church, acceptance of Mary decreased. As Mary's position decreased, religious and priestly vocations dwindled. It's all there. And we didn't need an apparition to define it for us (albeit we probably got one anyway at a place named Garabandal, which the ordained Church didn't want to hear about).

In only a fifteen year period, from 1960 to 1975, Marian devotion seemed to disappear. Much of the strength of the Catholic Church also seemed to disappear along with the Marian Movement. Seminaries and convents emptied. Schools closed. Vocations were lost. Mary was lost.

Strangely, in another short span of fifteen years, 1980 to 1995, the Marian Movement seemed to spring up again. This time though, it has become a period of wild and often-times uncontrolled reports of apparitions and supernatural manifestations. It has become an era of unprecedented visions, locutions, and claims of signs and wonders. Many seem to be of very suspicious origin.

What happened? How did this wild roller-coaster ride come about? Is the current difficulty in the Church the result of the fall of the Marian Movement? Or is it the other way around? Are all of these claimed apparitions of the past ten years for real? Was all of this caused by Vatican II as some would like to believe?

I wonder if we will ever know . . . or if it really makes any difference anyway? All of our salvation needs are covered in the Scriptures, and our Messiah has indeed come to open the gates to Paradise. The Paschal Mystery is duly recorded, and only Jesus will continue to be our Savior.

Still, the Marian Movement, like the Church, like the world in general, seems to be in some rather chaotic times.

The first scapegoat many of us look to whenever our spiritual goals and objectives seem to be drifting off course is Vatican II. All of the problems, it seems, can be traced back to that, claim some. And there is a mountain of evidence to support such a position. Nor does it really take another "Gallup Poll" to take the pulse of the faithful and to see where the Church is failing. Just look around.

On the other hand, the documents of Vatican II have not been locked away in a vault somewhere. Anyone can read them. And if you do read them, you may be shocked to find out just how "Marian" the Council was (so would some priests).

Chapter 8 of the *Constitution on the Church* was profoundly Marian. It was one of the longest chapters of all documents, over 3,500 words, and gave tribute to Mary in no uncertain terms. For example, #56 stated:

> "Rightly then do the Holy Fathers of the Church judge that Mary was not just employed by God in a passive way, but that she co-operated in human salvation by free faith and obedience. For she, as St. Irenaeus says, 'being obedient became a cause of salvation for herself and the whole human race.'"

That hardly sounds like the "Council Votes to Downgrade Mary" headlines that seemed to pop up around the country in October of 1963. In fact, so important was Mary's position in the Church to the participants of the Council, that they voted to include the schema on Mary into the major document on the Church as opposed to a separate document.

Number 62 of that document adds:

"This motherhood of Mary in the economy of grace continues unceasingly, from the consent which she gave in faith at the Annunciation, and which she unhesitatingly endured under the Cross, even until the eternal consummation of all the elect. For after she was assumed into heaven, she did not lay aside this role, but by her manifold intercession continues, winning the gifts (graces) of eternal salvation by her intercession. By her Motherly love, she takes care of the brothers of her Son who are still on the way to their eternal home and who are involved in dangers and difficulties, until they are led to the blessed fatherland. For this reason the Blessed Virgin is invoked in the church with the titles of Advocate, Auxiliatrix, Helper, and Mediatrix."

The same document, *Constitution on the Church*, had stated in #59:

After she was taken up, "she was exalted as Queen of the Universe by the Lord, so that she might be more fully conformed to her Son, the Lord of lords, and victor over sin and death."

The *Second Vatican Council* confirmed all previous dogmas, doctrines and titles given to Mary by previous Church councils, and officially named her as "Mother of the Church." Certain feast days were protected and confirmed as holy days of obligation. Specific liturgies were enacted for use throughout the year. She was honored throughout the documents of the Council, looked to for intercession constantly during the Council, and given a most special endorsement in the above referenced chapter in the *Constitution on the Church*.

Mary was downgraded? She was mentioned in 11 of the Council's 16 documents. Pope John XXIII, in announcing the Council, stated: "We must above all trust in the intercession of the Immaculate Mother of Jesus and our Mother for its success." The Pope began the first session on October

11th (feast of the Divine Maternity of Mary) and the first session of the Council ended on the feast of the Immaculate Conception, December 8th.

Pope Paul VI, successor to John XXIII, continued the Council, opening the new session with the reminder that "here certainly the Virgin Mother of Christ is helping us from Heaven." The above referenced major document of the Council was approved on November 21, 1964, the feast of the Presentation of Mary and on that same day the Pope proclaimed, to the world, that Mary is the *Mother of the Church*. In his address to the Council Fathers he also stated:

> "We wish that the Mother of God should be still more honored and invoked by the entire Christian people by this most sweet title."

Before the Council was to officially end, the Pope would also send a "golden rose" to the shrine at Fatima, a most high, symbolic, gesture of acceptance of what had happened there 47 years previously. The Pope would officially end the Council with still another special tribute to Mary, and if all of that wasn't enough, we can read the words of the conclusion of Mary's chapter in the *Constitution on the Church* where the Council Fathers stated:

> "This most Holy Synod deliberately teaches this Catholic doctrine and it admonishes all the sons of the Church that they should generously cultivate devotion, especially liturgical devotion, towards the Blessed Virgin, and that they should consider of great importance the practices and exercises of piety toward her that were recommended by the Magisterium of the Church over the course of centuries . . ."

Pretty strong words. Hardly a downgrade. How did the laity get so misinformed on what Vatican II actually stated? But perhaps the most outstanding and complete analysis of Mary's role in our lives and in the Church was published by the **National Conference of Catholic Bishops** in the United States, in 1973. We had made reference to, and recommended this document previously, but it is worthwhile mentioning again. *Behold Your Mother:Woman of Faith* is precise, positive, and very informative. Paragraph #93 bears quoting:

> "We view with great sympathy the distress our people feel over the loss of devotion to Our Lady and we share their concern that the young be taught a deep and true love for the Mother of God. We Bishops of the United States wish to affirm with all our strength the lucid statements of the Second Vatican Council on the permanent importance of authentic devotion to the Blessed Virgin, not only in the liturgy, where the Church accords her a most special place under Jesus her Son, but also in the beloved devotions that have been repeatedly approved and encouraged by the Church and that are still filled with meaning for Catholics. As Pope Paul has reminded us, the rosary and the scapular are among these tested forms of devotion that bring us closer to Christ through the example and protection of His Holy Mother."

But perhaps paragraph #92 of the Bishops' book is the most startling—one the ordained Church needs to take another look at. #92 states:

> "In writing this Pastoral Letter, our concern about our Lady is most keenly felt in the area of devotion. No survey is needed to show that all over the country many forms of Marian devotion have fallen into disuse, and others are taking an uncertain course. In an age avid for symbols (the peace medals and other signs of the young are evidence of this), the use of Catholic Marian symbols, such as the scapular and the Miraculous Medal, has noticeably diminished. Only a few years ago use of the rosary was a common mark of a Catholic, and it was customarily taught to children, both at home and in courses in religious instruction. Adults in every walk of life found strength in this familiar prayer which is biblically based and is

filled with the thought of Jesus and His Mother in the "mysteries." The praying of the rosary has declined. Some Catholics feel that there has even been a campaign to strip the churches of statues of our Lady and the saints. Admittedly, many churches were in need of artistic reform; but one wonders at the severity of judgment that would find no place for a fitting image of the Mother of the Lord."

It really makes you wonder if the Bishops actually ever read anything they write? Or adhere to it? Or many priests, who still think Mary is the imagination of those pious old ladies of the Legion of Mary! On the other hand, part of our answer to determining the place for Marian devotion in the Church can be found in one phrase of the above quoted paragraph #93. It says, "the permanent importance of authentic devotions . . ." We need to keep that word "authentic" in mind.

Something else happened in 1960 that had a profound effect on the Marian Movement. Or perhaps we should say something else didn't happen. What didn't happen was the long awaited disclosure of the famed third secret of Fatima. It was read by the Pope, and that was it. Millions of people, worldwide, who had been following Fatima for years, praying rosaries daily; promoting devotions in their parishes and in their homes; all of the Legion of Mary cenacles and other Marian groups; magazines and radio programs; all were suddenly just left in the lurch. Decades of stated importance; years of praying for Russia; and for the defeat of Satan (the St. Michael Prayer); repeated announcements of the promises of Fatima; and all tied to that portion of Our Lady's messages at Fatima that had never been revealed, seemingly just got dropped.

Another possible contributing factor was the elimination of certain Church Canons, and the establishment of others. A Canon Law of the early 1900s all but forbade the publishing or promotion of anything dealing with apparitions and private revelation. It was understandable given the upsurge of claimed visionaires following Bernadette of Lourdes, France, in 1858. Shortly after World War II, Cardinal Ottaviani, head of the *Congregation for the Faith*, produced guidelines and controls for the evaluation, investigation and promotion of apparitions and miracles that all but eliminated the possibility of any such supernatural phenomena ever gaining approval by the Church. In 1970, Pope Paul VI officially approved the removal of those Canons of the Church which prohibited the publishing of certain materials without an "Imprimatur." Shortly thereafter, Cardinal Seper, the successor to Cardinal Ottaviani, issued new guidelines for the evaluation of private revelation through apparitions, locutions, etc. They were approved in 1978. For better or for worse, a new explosion of visions and prophecy was about to occur. It had already begun through the rise of the Charismatic Renewal, a powerful and positive element in the lives of Christians, but which was also prone to exaggeration and the spin off into questionable groups and practices.

In any case, long standing Marian devotion had seen a sharp decline in the seventies, matching the decline in vocations. The Church was facing confusion and dissension; conservatives felt their spirituality was being replaced by peace and social justice issues; and the world was about to witness the greatest explosion of claimed apparitions it had ever seen. According to Father Bert Buby, renowned author in Mariology, the increasing number of alleged Marian apparitions is a sign of both world turmoil and confusion about Catholic teaching. "Whenever there is a period that is very disturbing in the history of humankind, or especially in the Catholic Church, the faithful often become confused and start searching for signs of divine intervention," Fr. Buby stated. He goes on to say that "in all cases, Church officials painstakingly study claimed apparitions, taking years, if necessary, before declaring a site worthy of veneration."

Well, that is sure open to some real contention. Today, it seems it is not only the faithful that are confused. As to the Church painstakingly studying all apparitions, if they really studied just 20% of the ones being promoted today, this book wouldn't be necessary.

Father Buby also noted that there is an excess of certain Marian devotions today, and the phenomena attributed to her. He also stated that part of the appeal of apparitions stems from the Church's inadequate presentation of Mary. Further, he noted that private apparitions tend to over-dogmatize Mary by going beyond even the dogmas of the Church. I, for one, say "Amen" to those three excellent observations by Fr. Buby.

But perhaps the "whys and wherefores" are not the most important issues.

This book is concerned with apparitions and the Marian Movement. If the book has any merit it is in the evaluation of the current status of each. The past is gone. The future is yet to come. The present is the issue and the fact that apparitions have gone out of control is the problem, and that is what we need to concentrate on. It means we need to let God be God, not a visionary.

CHAPTER 3

The Church and
Private Revelation

What is the Church's position on private revelation? We have already briefly identified her position on Mary, which certainly supports many of Mary's roles. But what about all these claimed appearances and messages? Stacy Mattingly, a writer from Atlanta, Georgia, states, "more Marian apparitions have been reported since 1981, when the Virgin Mary reportedly first appeared at Medjugorje, than during the whole of Church history." Well, that might be a little much, but still, reports of supernatural phenomena seem to be growing at an alarming pace today. With it comes a great interest in potential chastisement and the purification of the world, and of course the rather divided and confusing status of the Church and some of her teachings. A whole army of people have declared that they indeed have been chosen to be the new prophets of the world . . . some with a whole series of new teachings.

The Marian Movement has now reached a new crescendo, and claims of apparitions and heavenly messages are coming from everywhere giving both reasons for hope and predicted disasters. Have we taken over God's role? These are indeed exciting times. But is it all good? And first of all, are apparitions real? If they aren't we have to start all over from ground zero, including the Bible.

In the Bible that I use, *The New American Bible*, St. Joseph Edition, there are 1,468 pages. Do you know how many pages it takes before we get to our first apparition? It's on page six.

Page six out of almost fifteen hundred pages!

Just think; there are only two people in the world, and I'm a son-of-a-gun if they don't have an apparition. They couldn't even send a fax to anyone . . . or write a book about it. And it was a really neat message. Page six!

And guess what? It was wrong.

And you're still paying for it. Read *Genesis*, Chapter Three.

> *"You certainly will not die. No, God knows well that the moment you eat of it your eyes will be opened and you will be like gods who know what is good and bad."*

That's pretty powerful, and it certainly is a list of all positives. So what happened?

The woman ate the fruit, right?

No, wrong! She discerned. She discerned three things.

> *"The woman saw that the tree was good for food, was pleasing to the eyes, and desirable for gaining wisdom."*

So then she ate the fruit. And the whole thing was wrong. Page 6 out of over 1,400 pages. But there is some good news here as well. It only took six pages to show that apparitions and visions are real. They have been happening ever since.

Mary as well as St. Joseph were also recipients of visions. Both the Old and New Testaments contain accounts of numerous apparitions and supernatural manifestations. This is nothing new to Christianity in general, or even to the Jewish people of the Old Testament—from Abraham to the Apostles. Prophets also abound in Scripture and throughout the centuries, saints and doctors of the Church, the Hall of Fame of Church heroes, have left us their memoirs, teachings, diaries and literary works complete with testimonies of supernatural visits, visions and messages.

And what is the position of the Church regarding private revelation? Well, in spite of the above data confirming the reality of apparitions, the Church is not at all supportive or enthusiastic. There is worry about Catholics becoming too obsessive regarding a given apparition and/or its messages . . . and for good reason. Father Michael Miller, CSB, in his book, *"Marian Apparitions and the Church,"* states that "a piety that concentrates on Marian appearances can easily reduce one's religious life to a narrow devotionalism . . . can distract the faithful from the sacramental life of the Church . . . apparitions can become, to the follower, the true teacher of faith."

No doubt that for some the words of Mary to a visionary seem to replace those of Christ, or the Bible. Fr. Miller adds, "pastoral wisdom tells us that all too frequently some people seek false comfort in apparitions, counting on them to detail future events or easy ways to Heaven. . . . All the honor at a particular site given to Mary is owed to her as Mother of God. It should not be directed to her because she appeared at such a site. The locale is an occasion for veneration, not the reason for it. . . . Nor is Church approval an official statement that Mary definitely appeared to certain individuals. The burden of proof is always on those who claim the apparition is authentic."

It would seem that reasoning has much merit, especially when we recall that the first apparition the world got was a real bummer. In short, the Church contrasts the absolute certainty of Public Revelation, which she teaches in the name of God, and the relative uncertainty of private apparitions and revelations. The latter are but small news items in the life of the Church, the authenticity of which can only be established in a conjectural manner by a judgment which is always problematical.

Fr. René Laurentin, a leading Mariologist in the Church, listed four reasons for the extreme prudence the Church takes with apparitions:

1) Private revelation cannot add anything to Christ's Rev-

elation. We should not confuse Revelation (with a capital R) and what might better be called special or individual revelations.

2) Apparitions are "senses facts." That situates them at a very low level in respect to dogmas and knowledge of faith. Those signs which reach us through our senses always have a certain ambiguity.

3) Apparitions and private revelations are subject to illuminism, to illusions of subjectivity. The Church is therefore very prudent in this domain, having learned through centuries of experience.

4) Private revelation often gives umbrage to institutional authority; for common people can easily give more credence to seers who claim to have a direct connection to Heaven, than to the official authority of the Church which is mandated to speak the truth in the name of God. (Note: This one is a real biggie today.)

Fr. Laurentin also points out the various theologies of the Church involved in these studies: Dogmatic theology, Biblical theology, Fundamental theology, Moral theology, and Mystical theology. Please make special note of these above points. By the time you get to the **Conclusion** of this book, you will see the accuracy of his statements.

The new *Catechism of the Catholic Church* is not just a resource book or a reference book for a religious-ed teacher. It is the teaching of the Catholic Church. It has some specific things to say regarding apparitions. It would be good to read them. They begin on page 22 of the *Catechism*, beginning with #65. It specifically states that "God has said everything in his Word . . . He has spoken everything to us at once in this sole Word and he has no more to say." The *Catechism* emphatically states, "There will be no further Revelation." In part, #66 states:

> "The Christian economy, therefore, since it is the new and definitive Covenant, will never pass away; and no new public revelation is to be expected before the glorious manifestation of our Lord Jesus Christ."

The *Catechism* goes on to affirm the reality of certain

charisms of the faithful and the existence of apparitions and visions in stating:

> "Throughout the ages, there have been so-called private revelations, some of which have been recognized by the authority of the Church. They do not belong, however, to the deposit of faith. It is not their role to improve or complete Christ's definitive Revelation, but to help live more fully by it in a certain period of history . . . Christian faith cannot accept 'revelations' that claim to surpass or correct the Revelation of which Christ is the fulfillment."

The documents of *Vatican Council II* also strongly affirmed the existence of private revelation, but again reiterated the Church's position that such revelation can only be given human faith. The saints and doctors of the Church have also left us with some strong input regarding apparitions. We will be looking at some of those as well. But first it might be apropos to turn to the Bible. The big need with respect to private revelation is **to discern**. The need for discernment is the reason this book has been published. And the Bible gives us some definite guidelines.

The Biblical quotation usually given as a reference for the discernment process is covered in *Luke* 6:43-44, or *Matthew* 7:16-20, and 12:33. It states: *"you can tell the tree by its fruits."* Does the apparition bear good fruits? Frankly, that admonition is a little worn out. It is often presented as the standard to find acceptance for any claimed seer of heavenly messages. Any sign of good fruit whatsoever seems to guarantee authenticity. Church experience proves otherwise. First of all, there is a need to define "fruits." What seems like positive fruits sometimes prove contrary, especially after the initial throes of enthusiasm. So, the second problem appears to be a need for a specific time frame. Good fruits over how long a period of time? St. Ignatius tells us that Satan is most happy to provide us with very positive fruits (and he can), if in doing so he can capture our confidence and blow the whole thing up somewhere down the road. You also need to realize "good fruits" means the messenger as well as the message.

The Very Reverend Adolphe Tanquerey, and Reverend A. Poulain, S.J. each wrote a classic for the Church during their lifetime, dealing with mystical theology. We will quote from them throughout the rest of this book. In their studies and references to doctors of the Church dealing with private revelation there is a common thread throughout. Basically it says that Satan can and does deceive us by very willingly giving us 95% of absolute truth and goodness and light in some message, just to get us to also accept the other 5% that is not correct and that can do us in.

Still, private revelation is part of our faith and the Bible has some very definite things to say about it, both positive and negative. Scripture is very definitive in acknowledging that God does indeed speak to and through His people. It tells us that there has been and will be visions, and that old men will prophesy and young men will dream dreams. *"Do not stifle the Spirit. Do not despise prophecies. Test everything; retain what is good"* (*1 Thess.* 5:19-21). The Old Testament was filled with visions, angels, prophets, and miracles, and not all of them involved only God's people. The New Testament obviously offers more of the same, for the Savior is now on the scene. He eventually sends out His disciples to "do even greater things" than what He has done. Those gifts came in abundance with Pentecost as recorded in *Acts* 2:1-13:

> *"And suddenly there came from the sky a noise like a strong driving wind, and it filled the entire house in which they were. Then there appeared to them tongues as of fire ... and they began to speak in different tongues, as the Spirit enabled them to proclaim ... and all heard them speaking in his own language ..."* (*Acts* 2:1-13).

The apostles told the people to pursue these gifts and to further evangelize in the name of the Lord. *"Pursue love, but strive eagerly for the spiritual gifts, above all that you may prophesy ..."* (*1 Cor.* 14). And the Lord evidently responded to these good works: *"and when Paul laid his hands on them, the Holy Spirit came upon them, and they spoke in tongues and prophesied."* (*Acts* 19:16).

Vatican Council II, just as it did not "downgrade" Mary as some priests, bishops and theologians would have us believe, also did not downgrade private revelation and personal charisms. It certainly provided sound guidelines for following the teachings of the Church, but in #12 of the *Constitution on the Church* we read:

> "It is not only through the Sacraments and the ministries of the Church that the Holy Spirit sanctifies and leads the people of God and enriches it with virtues, but allotting His gifts to everyone according as He wills. He distributes special graces among the faithful of every rank. By these gifts He makes them fit and ready to undertake the various tasks and offices which contribute toward the renewal and building up of the Church. . . .
> "These charisms, whether they be the more outstanding or the more simple and widely diffused, are to be received with thanksgiving and consolation for they are perfectly suited to and useful for the needs of the Church."

Today, there appears to be a new wave of experts in mystical theology who openly pursue all claimed visionaries, patching together messages and prophecies from wherever and linking them together with Scriptural quotations and interpretations, mostly from the *Book of Revelation.* The end result is often another sensationalism approach to the coming chastisement and end times. But there are equally specific passages from the Bible that seldom get quoted and that are often overlooked totally. They outline the other side of the coin concerning private revelation and the dangers that abound. A very important sampling follows:

> *"Take care not to be misled. Many will come in my name saying 'I am he, and the time is at hand.' . . ."* (*Lk.* 21:8).
> *"For such people are false apostles, deceitful workers, who masquerade as apostles of Christ. And no wonder, for even Satan masquerades as an angel of light. So it is not strange that his ministers also masquerade as ministers of righteousness"* (*2 Cor.* 11:13-14).

1 Timothy, Chapter 1, warns against false doctrine and false teaching and states: *"Some people have turned to meaningless talk, wanting to be teachers of the law but without understanding the words they are using, much less the matters they discuss with such assurance."*

2 Timothy, Chapter 3, warns that we should *"understand this: there will be terrifying times in the last days. People will be self-centered and lovers of money, proud, houghty, abusive ... making a pretense of religion but denying its power. Reject them."* Most importantly, we have Chapter 4 of *Timothy* that seems so apropos for so many of today's claimed visionaries and apparition sites:

> *"The time will come when people will not tolerate sound doctrine, but, following their own desires, will surround themselves with teachers who tickle their ears. They will stop listening to the truth and will wander off to fables."*

Christ specifically told us *"you know not the day or the hour,"* so why all this concern over chastisement? The Bible also warns us that Satan can and does come "as an angel of light." The warnings against private revelation are stern indeed.

> *"First you must understand this: there is no prophecy contained in Scripture which is a personal interpretation. Prophecy has never been put forward by man's willing it. It is rather that men impelled by the Holy Spirit have spoken under God's influence."* (*2 Ptr.* 1:20-21).

> *"In times past there were false prophets among God's people, and among you also there will be false teachers who will smuggle in pernicious heresies ... Their lustful ways will lure many away. Through them, the true way will be made subject to contempt ... They will deceive you with fabricated tales, in a spirit of greed."* (*2 Ptr.* 2:1-3).

> *"If anyone says to you, then, 'Look, here is the Messiah!' or, 'There he is!' do not believe it. False messiahs*

and false prophets will rise and they will perform
signs and wonders so great as to deceive even the
elect ..." (*Matt.* 24:23-25)

Boy, that all seems like a whole lot of bad news but once again, all of the above referenced material, and all of the Biblical quotations shown, give rise to the need for discernment, and discernment is the first and foremost need today in the area of private revelation. And as we can see from all of the material listed in this book so far, it is usually a combination of encouragements and cautions, a list of difficult choices, and a large amount of "grey area" where answers are neither obvious nor certain. For those very reasons, and because of the fact that the Church (and most other Christian faiths as well) has steadfastly taught that there can be no further public revelation or change to the Bible as the inspired word of God, that need is all the more critical. There is one other power who is most aware of this, particularly in this age of supernatural manifestations, and his name is Satan.

Evidently it has usually been this way, at least since the time of Christ. The saints and doctors of the Church, especially those who have had personal experiences with private revelation, have had some profound things to say about it. Much of it bad. St. Ignatius, for example, provided us with his "Rules for the Discernment of Spirits" taken from the excellent book, *The Spiritual Exercises of St. Ignatius.* He tells us that it is a mark of the evil spirit to assume the appearance of an angel of light, and if the cause warrants, both the good angel and the evil spirit can give consolation to a soul. All the more reason for the need for strong discernment and less emotion. He also warns us as to confusion, division, anxiety, anger and fits of depression as being signs of a revelation not being from the right Spirit. Rev. A. Poulain, S.J. in his *The Graces of Interior Prayer* and St. Teresa of Avila also give us a series of rules or guidelines for the discernment of revelations. They are shown in the appendix of this book.

Included in the advice that Teresa of Avila, John of the Cross, Ignatius, and a host of others have given us is the caution to not be fooled by "signs and wonders" and the supposed "fruits." Fr. Poulain quotes extensively from the above listed saints and many others as well. In one account he recalls the plight of Magdalen of the Cross, a Franciscan Nun of the 16th century who early on had given herself to the devil. He promised her much. She entered the convent at age seventeen and was three times Abbess of her monastery. Aided by the demon, she simulated all the mystical phenomena you would ever want to see including ecstasy, levitation, the stigmata, revelations and prophecies repeatedly fulfilled. At the point where she believed she was near death, she confessed it all, implored the mercy of God and was exorcised.

St. Teresa of Avila and St. John of the Cross have some very negative things to say regarding apparitions. St. John stated: "Those things are not necessary means to the divine union and at times are rather obstacles, owing to our evil tendencies. Desire for revelations deprives faith of its purity, develops a dangerous curiosity which becomes a source of illusions, fills the mind with vain fancies, and often proves the want of humility and of submission to Our Lord who has already given us all that is needed for salvation." He also speaks harshly of spiritual directors who push the seers forward attaching more importance to these visions and falsely building up the person in the process. He states, "Some directors bid the person to pray to God to reveal to them such and such things concerning themselves or others."

St. Teresa, speaking of visionaries, states: "It happens that some of them are so weak an imagination, that whatever they think upon, they say they see it clearly, as it indeed seems to them; they also have so vigorous an understanding that they become quite certain of everything in their imagination."

St. John of the Cross further adds: "The devil rejoices greatly when a soul seeks after revelations and is ready to accept them; for such conduct furnishes him with many opportunities of delusions." St. Teresa adds: "When anyone can contemplate the sight of Our Lord for a long period of time, I do not believe it is a vision, but rather some overmastering idea." These two saints provide us with literally volumes of teachings on mystical theology, and they are obviously very hard on visionaries. With that said, let us recognize that they also were visionaries. Does that mean that they disqualify themselves?

St. Ignatius, in his **Rules for the Discernment of Spirits** states: "It is the part of the devil to transform himself into an angel of light to enter at the outset into the pious desires of the soul, and to end by suggesting his own designs. Thus when he sees a soul given to the practice of virtue, he firsts suggests sentiments in harmony with that soul's good dispositions." He adds, "As soon as the devil sees us to be humble, he strives to inspire us with a false humility, that is to say, an excessive vicious humility." St. Teresa adds to that by saying, "The devil frequently fills our thoughts with great schemes, so that instead of putting our hand to what work we can do to serve our Lord, we may rest satisfied with working to perform impossibilities." (What St. Ignatius and St. Teresa state in this paragraph seems very apropos today).

Let's add to all of that the knowledge that some of our most recognized saints have been prone to error in their teachings and literary works.

—St. Joan of Arc believed she would be saved from being burnt at the stake (from a vision).
—St. Norbert affirmed that he knew through revelation that the Antichrist would come in his generation (12th century).
—St. Vincent Ferrer spent the last twenty-one years of his life announcing that the Last Judgment was at hand. He was certain of the truth of it through a vision, and through many miracles he performed (Year 1400).
—The revelations of St. Bridget, St. Gertrude, and St. Catherine of Siena contradict each other in places.
—Catherine Emmerich, Mary of Agreda, St. Elizabeth of Schoenau, and St. Bridget all contradict each other as to when the Blessed Virgin Mary died.
—St. Bridget and Mary of Agreda (*Mystical City*) contradict each other with regard to the Nativity at Bethlehem.
—St. Colette said she had a vision indicating that St. Anne had been married three times.
—Historians and theologians have discovered many errors in the works of Blessed Anna Maria Taigi.

—A number of errors had been attributed to Mary of Agreda, to the extent that Clement XIV forbade her beatification in 1771.

—St. Catherine of Siena thought she had a vision where Our Lady stated that she was not immaculate.

—Catherine Emmerich had a symbolic vision showing that Mary of Agreda's works had been altered.

—Pope Leo X published a Bull prohibiting public prophecies by preachers.

—In 1872, as the result of a vast infusion of apparitions and prophecies, Pius IX attempted to quiet them all saying, "A large number of prophecies are in circulation, but I think that they are the fruit of the imagination."

—A number of items in the works of Mary of Agreda, attributed by her to "divine revelation" have been traced back to originating from other books.

—*Poem of the Man God* has been condemned, approved, accepted, rejected, verified, and disqualified, seemingly forever.

—Pope Benedict XIII, at the close of the great western schism (1420), was deposed. The story goes that he had relied on a vision from an Abbot who told him what the future would bring. Benedict supposedly based his decisions on this vision and it cost him his position on the pulpit.

The list is much longer. In any case, the above examples show that confusion in matters of private revelation is not limited to just our age. Seems like there were just as many questions throughout the centuries.

Adding to the above examples, *The Life of St. Catherine of Bologna* relates that the devil sometimes appeared to her in the form of the crucified Christ and demanded of her, under the appearance of perfection, the most impossible things in order to drive her to despair.

Pope Benedict XIV came down quite hard on visionaries of his day, stating: "What is to be said of those private revelations which the Apostolic See has approved of, those of the Blessed Hildegard, of St. Bridget and of St. Catherine of Siena? We have already said that those revelations, although approved of, ought not to, and cannot receive from us any assent of Catholic, but only human faith." Well, that may be, but some of the apparitions involving these "saints" were pretty dramatic. In the case of Mary of Agreda, she often times was seen "in levitation." What to make of it all! St. John of the Cross also stated that locutions should be avoided at all costs and no one should seek such things for the devil is looking for that type of soul. Regardless, Pope Benedict's statement on judging private revelation is still the official position of the Church today.

All a little disconcerting, wouldn't you say? But it is important that we can be assured that our era is not the only one in the history of the world that seems to be over-whelmed by private revelation—or the fear of chastisement. Still, it is very evident that these are very troubled times, albeit very exciting times; times when many people are bringing us some startling news they claim is from super-natural sources. And it's happening worldwide. With it comes a very strong responsibility to discern and there is great evidence that this process of discernment has been lacking, and in many cases non-existent.

There is an especially important word in the above sentence. It is **responsibility**. Discernment is not simply an option available to someone regarding whether to follow a claimed seer or not. Nor is it a process of acceptance based on whether your rosary turns gold at some apparition site or whether your camera was able to produce some magic photo, or whether we witness some solar phenomena. No question, that all helps in the process, but none of those things are representative of anything that the evil one can't do as well.

The *Code of Canon Law* indicates you not only have a right to speak out for your faith, but an obligation to do so. It also specifically states what the obligations of bishops are, not just their authority. Canon law also applies to your rights and duties. The documents of Vatican II outline many of these same points. Some interesting excerpts from the *Code of Canon Law*:

> Canon #209: "The Christian faithful are bound by an obligation, even in their own patterns of activity, always to maintain communion with the Church."

Canon #212 includes the statement: "In accord with the knowledge, competence and preeminence which they possess, the Christian faithful have the right and even at times a duty to manifest to the sacred pastors their opinion on matters which pertain to the good of the Church . . ."

Canon #213: "The Christian faithful have the right to receive assistance from the sacred pastors out of the spiritual goods of the Church, especially the word of God and the sacraments."

Canon #229: "Laypersons are bound by the obligation and possess the right to acquire a knowledge of Christian doctrine adapted to their capacity and condition so that they can live in accord with that doctrine, announce it, defend it when necessary, and be enabled to assume their role in exercising the apostolate."

That all sounds pretty specific. What about the ordained Church, and specifically the bishops and theologians? Some quick references:

Can. #386: The diocesan bishop is bound to present and explain to the faithful the truths of the faith which are to be believed and applied to moral issues, frequently preaching in person; he is also to see to the careful observance of the prescriptions of the canons concerning the ministry of the word, especially those concerning the homily and catechetical formation, so that the whole of Christian doctrine is imparted to all.

Through suitable means he is strongly to safeguard the integrity and unity of the faith to be believed while nevertheless acknowledging a rightful freedom in the further investigation of its truths.

Can. #392: Since he must protect the unity of the universal Church, the bishop is bound to promote the common discipline of the whole Church and therefore to urge the observance of all ecclesiastical laws.

He is to be watchful lest abuses creep into ecclesiastical discipline, especially concerning the ministry of the word, the celebration of the sacraments and sacramentals, the worship of God and devotion to the saints, and also the administration of property.

Can. #748: All persons are bound to seek the truth in matters concerning God and God's Church; by divine law they also are obliged and have the right to embrace and to observe that truth which they have recognized.

The laity have specific responsibilities as well as rights within the Church. So do priests and bishops. In all cases those responsibilities include defending the Church and the faith, and making certain that the faithful in the Church receive proper and true teaching. Parts of the *New Catechism of the Catholic Church* cover these aspects just as the *Code of Canon Law* does. For example, Catechism chapters include:

#874 to 896—Bishops and hierarchy of Church
#897 to 950—the laity
#964 to 975—The Blessed Virgin Mary
#65 to 73—Private revelation

Combining the Bible, The Code of Canon Law, the documents of Vatican II, and the New Catechism of the Catholic Church, there are hundreds of pages that provide input and direction that would include private revelation. It indicates that both the ordained Church as well as the laity have a strong responsibility to search out truth in this period of wild and overwhelming prophecy, visions and revelations. It includes the fact that only God can be God.

We also have to recognize here that some who read this book and are prone to follow certain private revelations today will view this mountain of data as being very judgmental, if not detrimental.

Discernment is difficult enough without getting it entangled in the "judgment" web. Discerning and judging are two different words with very similar meanings. The first need, then, is to define them. Discerning speaks of: a perception, a judgment, a insight or ascertaining. Judgment speaks of: an opinion or estimate, the act of deciding, an examination or testing, discerning of criterion.

Obviously, the two words are running together, and both definitions are supported by the Church in her teachings, and by the Scriptures; and in neither case are the definitions speaking of condemnation or slander. Let's take that and go back and look at that statement again made by Our Lord, and the oft quoted sentiment that Jesus never "judged" anyone. Perhaps so. But He sure laid out the scribes and Pharisees pretty good on a number of occasions, and referred to them as a "brood of vipers." There are some other passages that perhaps we should evaluate as well that appear judgmental.

John the Baptist (in *Luke*, Chapter 3) was more than judgmental as he condemned the activity of Herod with his brother's wife. *Ezekiel*, Chapter 3:17-21 refers to the fact that the Lord will actually hold you responsible for the death of someone who had committed some wicked deed because you did not warn him. "*Reprimand publically those who do sin, so that the rest also will be afraid,*" says *1 Timothy*, Chapter 5:20. *Matthew*, Chapter 18, tells us of the grave consequence of "causing one of these little ones to sin," but it goes on to tell us that indeed we are our brother's keeper."

> "*If your brother sins against you, go and tell him his fault between you and him alone. If he listens to you, you have won over your brother. If he does not listen, take one or two others along with you ... if he refuses to listen to them, tell the church*" (18:15-17).

The Gospel of *Luke*, Chapter 10, is either very judgmental or is involved in some heavy duty discerning depending on your point of view. Actually, condemnation might be a more accurate word. "*Woe to you, Chorazin! Woe to you, Bethasaida! ... it will be more tolerable for Tyre and Sidon at the judgment than for you ... as for you Capernaum, You will go down to the netherworld.*" The 11th Chapter of *Luke* is a whole lot of "*woes to you*" and the Lord is very definitive in what He is saying. In Chapter 12:50-59, He calls the crowd hypocrites and tells them to "*judge for yourselves.*"

Judgmental or not, one point is of prime importance here. Regarding private revelation discernment is vital, and if one wishes to call that judgmental, so be it. That one, prime, important point is simply that it is not the Church we are discerning. It is not Scripture, not Church Doctrine, not the Pope nor the Magisterium of the Church, not some saint or doctor of theology. It's simply a fellow human being who is claiming some special connection with the Lord, His Mother, or with Heaven, or who is claiming he or she has some special insight as to the future.

Maybe they do. But we better be sure. Our faith may be at stake. Or our soul. The burden of proof is always on the claimed seer or mystic. We are never obligated to believe any private revelation, Lourdes and Fatima included.

Discernment: The Process, The Problems

Those of us who have been heavily involved in the Marian Movement are fully aware of the position of the ordained Church from the 1930s to the 1970s. Private revelation was all but squashed by Cardinal Ottaviani and the *Congregation for the Doctrine of Faith* in Rome. The *Code of Canon Law* also severely restricted the publication of anything relating to these issues, and an *"Imprimatur"* was a steadfast requirement in any case.

Many believe some credible private revelations have been lost over the past fifty or sixty years because of these sanctions. The very renowned Marian theologian, Fr. René Laurentin has stated that Lourdes would never have been approved if it had occurred during this period of time. Some question that assessment. Are we to believe that God is limited to the instruments of communication that only mankind has devised? Or to man made laws? Is the Lord going to require the permission of mankind, before He can return as He promised? The faith has spread around the world over a period of many centuries. And with it went the communication of miracles, visions, healings, conversions, and what have you, and mostly without TV cameras, fax machines, electronics, even phones or the printed word. Lourdes generated millions of pilgrims, as did Fatima, and long before any of these modern communications were available, and regardless of whether anyone knew the Code of Canon Law or not. It will always be so, albeit the Lord seems to prefer to work within our human limitations if at all possible (thank God). On the other hand, He doesn't need to.

In any case, Canons #1385 and #2318 were abolished (along with the need for an *Imprimatur*) and this action officially approved by Pope Paul VI in October of 1970. Cardinal Seper succeeded Cardinal Ottaviani as head of the *Congregation for the Faith*, and on February 25, 1978, he issued a four page document on the norms for judging presumed apparitions and revelations. The appendix of this book includes several different guidelines for the discernment of apparitions, including the basics of Cardinal Seper's document.

In any case, eliminating those Canons meant the floodgates opened and in the 26 years since 1970, hundreds of apparitions and new private revelations were reported.

Still, the criteria of the Church in evaluating apparitions has not and probably will not change. It is always conjectural. An apparition is still just a small news item in the life of the Church, a sensible manifestation of Christ, or the Blessed Virgin, or some other being from the beyond. It is difficult and problematic to judge. Is it really Christ or the Virgin? Is it an illusion, a deceitful trick of someone, or of the devil?

The "process" of discerning private revelations, the formal process, is being relegated to the appendix here. It is pretty well spelled out, as to what needs to be done, how, and by whom. And, all of that **primarily** needs to be accomplished by the ordained Church.

The need here is more directed to the laity and the "problems" being encountered. As has often been mentioned by Fr. Laurentin, as well as a number of other noted authors, the *sensus fidelium* is paramount to judging any private revelation—and will usually be right. If no one ever went to Lourdes or Fatima, why would the Church have had to get involved to begin with? What would there be to evaluate? If there were no healings, no conversions, no messages, no spiritual fruits, why bother? It is the faith of the people who necessitate this action. It is also the faith of the people which drives the Marian Movement. Though devotion to the Blessed Virgin Mary has always been led by special devout sons or daughters in the ordained Church, or by Popes specifically dedicated to Our Lady, it is the faithful laity who have always promulgated the activity and the devotions, and who have been, and currently are, on the frontlines of the apparition and private revelation phenomena.

They are also the least supported or heard by the Church hierarchy. Unfortunately, they are also the least involved in attempting to discern all that is being claimed.

Many of us now seem to play some part in adding to the confusion of already difficult issues. Ordained Church leaders, who are responsible for guidance and direction in these areas, are often nowhere to be found. Over zealous critics and supporters tend to either condemn or support everything. The process of discerning is that ground in the middle which desperately needs to be controlled.

For example, Fr. Albert J. Hebert, S.M. represents that portion that is in favor. Fr. Albert has given his life to the Church, and to Our lady, and is an accomplished author, but he seems to have seldom found an apparition he didn't like, or a visionary he didn't believe in. For example, in his book *"The Discernment of Visionaries and Apparitions Today,"* Father Al states:

> In all of this, numerous apparitions and private revelations occurring throughout the world, play a vital and important part for both Church and World. It is most necessary and most urgent that the many authentic revelations (in the minds of many experts in this field, as also in the convictions of multitudes of the faithful—*sensum fidelium*!) be approved ecclesiastically as soon as possible. Delays, especially long delays will bring any decisions too late. They will prevent the many graces which God wants for all people through apparitions He has brought about, and which He wants His Church to approve; and not to make His Will void."

That is a pretty generic approval of claimed visionaries. It also stated that the Church basically just gets in the way of these things, and that the Church cannot in any way restrict the rights of anyone to visit, support, or believe in any apparition whether it is condemned or not. He also states that even where errors are proven in certain aspects of some private revelation, "one can depend upon the *substance* of the revelation . . ." (Whoops!) The book goes on to insinuate that many priests and bishops are "anti-Mary" (probably true), and believe anything Marian is off-center. He endorses all claimed seers' publications stating, "what Christ or Mary want published, one should fear not to publish it, or to subject its release to undue delay." I would think all of that is not in the best interest of the Marian Movement today, or of the Church.

On the other hand, there are priests who are only too eager to condemn all apparition sites or seers. Medjugorje is a favorite target. Such would be Ivo Sivric, OFM, or Vittorio Guerrera, and certain publications such as *The Remnant* or *Fidelity Magazine* where Michael Jones has written extensively on Medjugorje.

The Marian Movement (read supporters of apparition sites), is chastized by the left or liberal element as being too out dated and hung-up on pre-vatican II devotion, and by the conservative right as being too fanatical and apparition chasers. For example, Louise DeAngelo, while writing the introduction for a book titled, *Medjugorje: A Closer Look*, painted a rather pathetic picture of anyone following apparitions. While making some very excellent points regarding the excesses involved, she nonetheless provides a lot of ridicule. That appears to be pretty common as critics seem to want to label believers of apparitions as some kind of demented, fanatical followers of claimed seers who are all either evil, frauds, or unbalanced. Probably the exact opposite is true. The Marian Movement in general, and the private revelation aspect in particular, seem to be a mirrored image of the problems in the Church today in general. The only real need is direction and guidelines.

While there are obvious dangers in supporting Fr. Hebert's position that new devotions, sacramentals, or new revelations and publications all have merit, he also makes some very strong points as to past errors in the discernment process of the Church. Other notable authors, such as Rene Laurentin, Karl Rahner, and the famed Father Garrigou-Lagrange have done so as well and bear listening to. They point out that Joan of Arc was the victim of some false accusations, as was Francis of Assisi and Alphonsus Liguori.

More known in our own time, how about visionaries such as Blessed Sister Faustina and Padre Pio. They were terribly sanctioned by the Church and declared not worthy of belief. They were obviously (along with Sr. Lucia) the prominent mystics of our time, and both now are in the process of reaching sainthood.

As to new devotions or revelations, there again are many examples that give credence to support those claims. Such was the revelations of Jesus to St. Margaret Mary Alacoque concerning devotion to the Sacred Heart, and the visions of St. Catherine Laboure and Bernadette regarding the Immaculate Conception and the Miraculous medal. Today, devotion to the Divine Mercy (Sr. Faustina) is worldwide and Divine Mercy Sunday is celebrated by the Church the first Sunday after Easter, and this after Faustina's works were originally opposed by the Church.

It is far too late to dispute apparitions, visions, prophecies, and messages. We are simply way past that. They are real, they are happening now, and whether we all wish to believe it—or not—some of the current crisis in the world and in the Church seems tied to them. No one can get them out of the Bible or the Church any more than they can get the Blessed Virgin Mary out. The need then, is not to try to blow them all up, but discern which are authentic and try to use them for our benefit. There are obviously some frauds; some emotionally ill; some being deceived; and some which are authentic. God's ways are not our ways. He can choose whomever He wishes . . . and has.

Both the Old Testament and New Testament had believers and non-believers involved in signs and wonders. The Old Testament is replete with prophets and special servants of God, often those we might consider least likely to be asked to work in a special way for Him. The New Testament, too, gives witness to God's designs to pick and choose at His discretion.

So apparitions and visions, like many of those currently being reported of the Blessed Virgin Mary, are an integral part of our faith. The phenomena themselves are very possible, so their reality cannot be disputed outright. Since the close of Public Revelation, it still continues—signs and wonders, miracles, cures, visions, prophecies, including

various charismatic gifts. Many people rightly question
these reports and are uncomfortable with the possibility of
their existence.

History has proven that the Father of Creation often
chooses to manifest His interest in our lives. At the same
time, His adversary has much power and will attempt to
undermine any loving efforts on God's part. Shouldn't these
facts be at the forefront of any discussion of supernatural
phenomena?

Once the certainty and reality of visions, prophecy, and
other supernatural manifestations has been recognized, we
can then recognize who else has also been the producer of
such things. Satan can and does provide all of those same
signs and wonders. He even tempted the Christ, not to mention all of the disciples, saints and leaders of the Church
down through the centuries. Some of the leading saints,
doctors, and theologians of the Church have recorded (complete with witnesses) many such occurrences for us. Padre
Pio even suffered physical assault from the devil in return
for all of the souls he was saving.

Spoon benders, mind readers, seances, clairvoyants,
magicians, mystics and prophets. Do you really doubt that
Satan can produce his own cadre of mystics? What about
Edgar Cayce? What about the evil Rasputin who seemingly
had unexplainable powers? What about the prophecies of
Nostradamus, or even certain claimed Catholic mystics?
What about voodoo witch doctors and high priests of various Asian and far eastern sects that can invoke some
higher spirit, producing strange but true results. These
manifestations are now shown on television regularly,
good and evil spirits all linked together, guaranteeing us of
some higher power, some other universe, some other alien
being, some other great force . . . but never a guarantee of
Jesus.

Today, we can add another dimension called the New Age
Movement. It also can and does produce some amazing, unexplainable phenomena and is interwoven into many various aspects of Christian beliefs. It promotes miracles,
healings, supernatural beings, a God (the hierarchy of Masters), future life, peace, joy, and a whole bunch of good stuff.
Right now the New Agers are up to their ears in promoting

angels and the Blessed Virgin Mary. Make no mistake about it, Mary and angels are very hot topics. They can generate much interest, and produce many $$$.

You will very rarely see any New Age promotion that does not come across as strongly positive. Light, goodness and peace are usually present. As stated in the Bible, Satan can and does come as an angel of light. And that is exactly where the New Age comes from. It is a religion. It's beginnings are found in the Bible, *Genesis* 3:5, and Satan is its supreme being. There are many books available, written by gurus in the New Age Movement which verify this fact while promoting the New Age agenda.

Once again, it is all just more material to justify the tremendous and urgent need to discern the supernatural manifestations happening everywhere today. There is a need for us to recognize the fact that most claimed apparitions have been infiltrated, that there has been an intermingling of spirits, and you may be bucking heads with a spirit much stronger than you are. Think! Question! Discern.

If you can accept the fact that Satan really exists (and you are at odds with the Catholic Church and most other Christian faiths as well, if you don't accept it), where do you think Satan would rather direct his utmost efforts: toward those who don't recognize his reality, or who are no threat to him; or would his efforts produce better results if he could get right in there with those faith-filled, church goers and really divert some souls with some really neat sounding messages and prophecies?

We know we are dealing with major issues here when the media and secular press start raising their un-believing eyebrows. Take note of all of the documentaries on TV during the past decade dealing with the supernatural, miracles, angels, visions, evil, unexplainable disasters and weather changes, etc. etc. In November, 1995, *Newsweek* magazine ran a major article by Kenneth Woodward on the vanishing face of sin in our society, and with it, the corresponding need to question the existence of an evil being. The article states that what used to be considered vices in our world— pride, cunning, greed and self-assertion—became virtues required for survival. Woodward goes on to point out that "if the Devil has died to American culture, perhaps it is because we no longer see in his myth, the image of our own worst inclinations."

That seems all too logical. But we need to also apply the "Satan myth" to the Marian Movement, and in particular, to the realm of apparitions and all private revelation. If the message is good, if the words ring true, if there is evidence of positive fruits, if there are signs and wonders, then it can't be wrong. It can't be from Satan! Right?

Wrong! It could be from Satan. Discern. Read *Genesis* 3:4-5 again. He is not a myth. He can deceive.

Then read from the *Book of Revelation*, Chapter 12. The Bible begins and ends with the Blessed Virgin Mary. She is there throughout. She is an arch-enemy of this fallen angel, this father of lies, this master of deceit. The Church has long recognized that Satan's greatest achievement would be to destroy the Church from within. To some, he is doing his job well today. But he has always been up against that army of devotees of "The Woman Clothed With the Sun," his arch-enemy. He has long believed if he could eliminate that army, the foundation of the Church would collapse. And he's probably right! What easier way than to infiltrate this enormous craze over private revelation! And the workings of Satan can be *"accompanied by all the power and signs and wonders at the disposal of falsehood . . ."* (2 *Thess.* 2:9).

One of the initial problems is simply the fact that many of those who tend to believe the current crop of claimed visionaries can not and will not listen to any critique or warning. **Remember, judging can also be defined as a form of discerning and warning.** We probably need to be a little more conservative here in our approach.

For example, one Catholic clergyman, a staunch supporter of most current, claimed seers has stated:

> "There are some ignorant, sanguine, rose-colored glasses type of people who disbelieve or condemn **authentic** visionaries because these unbalanced critics see only the warning or 'gloom' side of admonitions and some prophecies. The **Old Testament** and part of the **New**, including the very important **Apocalypse** [his emphasis], are full of dire warnings and prophecies."

Wow! That's a little heavy. I for one don't consider myself "ignorant, sanguine, or disbelieving," though some may think I am "unbalanced," but still, we probably need to provide a little more "balance" as well to his statement. First and foremost, those dire warnings and prophecies as mentioned happen to be in the Bible, not just passed out on some street corner, albeit some street corner preaching has produced good results.

Vatican II, in *"Lumen Gentium,"* Chapter 12, tells us that these kinds of gifts of grace "must be accepted with gratefulness and consolation, as they are specially suited to, and useful for, the needs of the Church. . . ." But it also tells us "judgments as to their genuineness and their correct use lies with those who lead the Church and those whose special task is not to extinguish the spirit but to examine everything and keep what is good."

St. Thomas Aquinas told us that in every period of the Church "there have been persons possessed of the spirit of prophecy, not to set forth new doctrines, but to give direction to human actions." Cardinal Ratzinger confirmed that, as well as the crescendo of current claimed apparitions, in his book *The Ratzinger Report.* He stated that one of the signs of our times is indeed the announcements of Marian apparitions multiplying all over the world. But he also cautioned that it is vitally important for us to "separate the aspect of the true or presumed supernaturality of the apparitions from that of its spiritual fruits." That gets into discernment, and discernment is the part of the whole apparition picture that is missing.

We have probably covered enough material in this book at this point to be able to arrive at a rather obvious conclusion:

> Today, activity within the Marian Movement (read devotion to the Blessed Virgin Mary) is being reduced to largely the pursuit of apparitions and messages.

As far as the last decade of this century is concerned, the above statement seems to be pretty accurate. Claims of heavenly messages are coming from everywhere. It has reached a crescendo. These are indeed exciting times, the era of Our Lady as proclaimed by Pope John Paul II some six years ago, when he announced a new "Marian Year." He told us Our Lady was ushering in the advent of a new millennium.

Undeniable things are happening. A merciful God is calling to His people. Conversions abound at some apparition sites and we have all seen renewal take place in the hearts of so many. With that said, we need to recognize the existence of the other side of the coin. It is the darker side, the one wrought with problems and these difficulties of discernment. Satan is right in the middle of everything, and to add to the confusion, many no longer believe he even exists.

Isn't it truly amazing? There is almost universal consensus that troubles abound in our society today, that the family is a vanishing value, that violence, drugs, sex and death are the hallmarks of our society. And yet, so many people want to believe that Satan is only the Bogey-man, a fictitious figure with a tail and carrying a pitch-fork. Where do they think all that evil comes from? To some it is just a metaphor for very bad luck. In this "New Age," whose religion is often based on pride of self, there is no room for a devil. If we have truly lost our sense of sin, there is little need to believe in Satan.

Perhaps equally amazing (and puzzling) is our pre-occupation with the "end times." To some that means the end of the world. To some it means the end of an era. Some even feel like it's the beginning of the dreaded chastisement, the three days of darkness, the era of evil before the peace of Christ reigns. The puzzling part of it is hinged on "too much credibility" being given too many visionaries and their prophecies of purification, and "too little credibility" being given to the possibility that Satan could somehow be involved in at least some of this. It's shown in the absolute acceptance some of us can give to a rosary changing color, or a magic photo, as being **proof** of someone's or someplace's authenticity, and being able to totally reject any idea of there ever being any evil connected with it in any way.

Then, add to that, the notion that many of these same prophecies include severe chastisement from our God for our sins, our rejection of His grace, and our supposed acceptance of the lies of Satan—you know, the one who doesn't exist. Thus the rapidly expanding belief that we are in the end times, and that chastisement is upon us.

Well it definitely is. Not because some visionary says so, but because Jesus says so. The Bible says so. The Church says so. That is all part of our faith. It is part of Catholic Doctrine. And you don't need a visionary to tell you that. In fact, even the new *Catechism of the Catholic Church* tells us that, in paragraphs #668 to #678. It is all a confirmation of the Scriptures. The Scriptures we must believe. Private revelation is simply a matter of choice.

The end times and the chastisement were forecast many centuries ago. Its reality came from the result of the efforts of you-know-who in the garden of Eden. We're still fighting it out. Regardless, what are you going to do about it anyway?

The Church does not believe you need to sell your stocks, cash in your insurance policies, hide your money under your mattress, pray new devotions for hours each day and finally, move to such and such a refuge center. The Church's teaching on this subject has never changed and continues to reflect the very words of Jesus:

You know not the day or the hour.

We all face a form of chastisement—our own end times. None of us will ever leave this earth alive. How or when or where that happens is not important. The only chastisement you have to fear then, is spiritual. It is the battle for your soul.

The Church, the Bible, the Documents of Vatican II, the New Catechism, the doctors and saints and traditions of our faith, have all said yes to the reality of Mary, and of apparitions. The Church has also provided the guidelines on how to deal with these issues. We need to act on them. For several reasons, we have apparently been reluctant to do so. In the past ten years probably two hundred visionaries have surfaced, over 50 in the United States alone. Hundreds of "message books" and topics have been printed or produced containing all kinds of predictions, revelations, devotions and warnings. Videos, pictures, statues, chaplets, anything and everything is now being made available concerning appearances of Mary. Our Lady has become a multi-million dollar business.

It is now becoming obvious that some of it has become

infiltrated, and some of it is simply not true. There is an urgent need for people involved in Marian devotion to hear the facts, the other side of the coin regarding some of these claims. There has also been a reluctance to do so up to this point. Critics have seemed to only concentrate on a specific apparition site (usually Medjugorje), or have been content to scuttle them all. Supporters often seem to embrace them all.

I honestly have no interest in becoming the martyr or folk-hero in all of this. I claim no authority in taking either the Church's position, or that of any claimed seer, and do not claim to be an expert in private revelation. In fact, I don't believe there are any experts. I'm doing this book because no one else has and because it is needed.

As far as current visionaries go—and I'm talking about this country—I do **not** support approximately 75% of them. If you do, then fine. But it should not be simply based on false hope, or heart-felt emotion, or fear of going against Jesus or His Mother. I will attempt to show you why I do not support the 75%. Many will take the position of: "how dare you say something against so-and-so. I have been there; I have witnessed the signs and wonders—rose petals falling, the sun spinning. I know of healings."

Some will believe this book even adds confusion and dis-sension to the entire area of private revelation, that it is pro-viding nothing positive, only negative. That is completely understandable, and I can see why someone would feel that way. On the other hand, I think that before you finish with this book you will become very aware of the following:

1) Confusion in the area of private revelation is already there—everywhere.

2) This book is not published to spread the clouds of gloom and doom, but to do the opposite. The doom and chastisement is already there—everywhere.

3) There is no need to simply attempt to expose some visionary or questionable apparition site. They are doing that themselves—everywhere. The objective here is to promote discernment and caution through examples already available—everywhere.

And there is certainly a need to present the positive side. We will attempt to do that as well. I believe in private revelation, in prophecy, visions, and gifts of the Holy Spirit. Today, as throughout Church history, there is a lot of positive things to say about both Marian devotion and private revelation. We urgently need to protect that. It is vital to the Church.

But, since we will try to finish this book on a positive note, detailing the pluses and hopefully providing some possible solutions, we will look at the questionable, or the "bad news" first.

A Short Analysis

The 1978 guidelines put out by the Vatican for the judging of apparitions provides some pretty specific directions. They are covered in quick summary form here, and more fully in the appendix of this book.

The first point noted in the document, and most importantly, acknowledges that reports of apparitions spread very rapidly today because of the existing communication advancements. In light of this, bishops are advised to rapidly make a pronouncement clarifying the status of a claimed apparitions. That obviously is the first problem in that this is seldom done.

The initial clarification requested of the bishop involved is:

Has the supernatural quality of the apparition been established at this point, or has the **non**-supernatural quality of the claimed apparition been established. The first says "we don't know yet" (Medjugorje). The second says "we don't accept it." The first expresses a doubt, perhaps. The second excludes the doubt and closes the question.

The document goes on to identify positive and negative criteria to look for. Positive criteria includes:
* Sound devotion and rich spiritual fruits.
* Theological and spiritual doctrine being true and free from error. No new revelations being claimed.
* Certainty, or at least great probability as to the existence of the facts and that it all happened.
* Personal qualities of those involved. (And this point is very important).
   Negative criteria includes:
* Manifest error as to the fact or facts presented.
* Doctrinal error.
* Immoral or other sinful actions of the person(s) involved.

* Evident seeking of financial advantage.
* Lack of humility, obedience to the Church, and in turn, seeking fame or publicity.
* Any form of mental illness or psychosis.

The second and third parts of the document outline the steps for the local bishop to pursue, as well as the responsibilities and rights of the faithful in the matter. Additionally, it provides steps for the local Ordinary to take to generate regional or national evaluation, or for bringing the authority of the Holy See into the investigation. The fifth and final part of the document outlines the role of the *Congregation for the Doctrine of the Faith* in the matter, and how this can be implemented if so requested.

It is also important to note that there are two distinctions made in the evaluation of apparitions. First, the recognition of the **devotions** can be approved if sound and beneficial to the faithful. Second, the **apparitions** themselves. It seems to have a lot to do with the Church's practice of placing great importance on the *"Sensus fidelium"* in matters of private revelation. Therefore, if the bishop takes action on some claimed site, it is because the faithful have gone there, have given some credence to it (or not), and have provided the bishop with some reason to become involved. As a result, there is nothing in the 1978 document from the Holy See that says that the faithful must wait and not visit a certain site, or take any action on it until the Church has recognized it. Nor does it state that an apparition cannot be approved (or deposed) until the event has ceased.

Finally the document lists certain responsibilities of the faithful in these matters, and like all of the aforementioned, these responsibilities seem lacking in the hotbed of apparitions today. Pope Benedict XIV provided the definitive statement on private revelation, a position still adhered to by the Church. It, like further information on the discernment of apparitions is shown in the appendix herein.

In much simpler terms, what follows here is an **unofficial** check list for the discernment of messages. The reader needs to recognize the fact that though these guidelines have been "borrowed" from materials approved by the Church and re-stated in simple, modern day terms, still, I am not the authority of the Church in these matters and it is a list I composed. I totally submit to the judgment of the Church in the event that any item on the following list is not in keeping with accepted doctrine.

Additionally, in the appendix section of this book, there are several specific visionary/apparition situations in the United States that are shown in detail as examples for the need of this kind of discernment.

Red Flags and Warnings

We should all give special attention to messages and message books and tapes that include a number of the following elements. At the same time, we need to accept the fact that any visionary, like ourselves, is not infallible. Thus, we are looking for a number of the following ingredients inherent in the material, not just a single item of concern:

—Messages that oppose priests, bishops, and aspects of Church Doctrine or liturgies. Included are those that claim to introduce new doctrines, or additional revelation to be added to the Scriptures.

—Messages that seem to be based on sensationalism, with too much purification and chastisement. Messages that suggest the Lord (or His Mother) is calling us names, threatening and putting down our faith or our efforts.

—Messages that specifically address politicians, important dignitaries, or that give economic and social advise, including philosophy, commerce and elections.

—Messages that specifically identify third parties (a biggie today), even fourth parties; messages that condemn them, admonish them, or glorify them, or direct these parties to do such and such.

—Messages that appoint people to positions in certain ministries, or that give people certain titles and authority.

—Messages that promote visionaries, provide indications of power, status, profit, position, publicity; those that seem to promote pride instead of humility.

—Messages that seem to indicate the end of God's mercy and that Jesus' salvific mission was a failure.

—Messages that create confusion and dissension within their own circle of influence, or within other organizations, parishes, apparition sites, or as to the position of the Church in the matter.

—Messages that show consistent contradiction (very big today and very important). These messages will include contradiction from page to page, or from segment to segment. The seer is alternately beat up by the Lord, then praised. "Hurry and get this book printed." Next, it is: "Don't worry, I will take care of everything." "Spend time with your kids." "Spend all your time with Me. Only I am important." etc. etc.

—Messages that promote new devotions and such an abundance of prayer so as to make your normal day impossible.

—Messages that seem to be overly stressing the publication of books, distribution of the messages, regardless of what position the Church might take. Messages that indicate the publishing of the book is what's important, not the seeking of a spiritual advisor or the blessing of the Church.

—Messages that are too caught up in outside interests: books, films, buy land, build a refuge center, a new community, move here, go there, start this organization, etc.

—Messages that seem to add new dimensions to Jesus, or to Mary. These would be messages where Jesus or Mary seem more interested in their own accomplishments than the promotion of the Good News. Such as their announcements of: My books, my farm, my house, my ministry, my success, my power, my authority, and those messages that seem like Jesus, or His Mother are really interested in building some sort of gigantic, highly successful, earthly empire.

—Any message that seems likely to strip a visionary of humility and obedience, and replace it with ego and power.

—Coupling apparition sites and events to specific messages. There may be a need to stay away from those that seem to have—or need—a message from Jesus or Mary for every single decision and action that happens, or that is desired to happen.

—Messages that are geared to prophecies, usually of doom and destruction, suggesting dates or places, but are repeatedly wrong.

At this point, please make a note to read from the Bible, preferably before proceeding to Chapter IV of this book. The passage to be read is only one page. It is *2 Timothy*, Chapter 4. It discusses false prophets and in part, states:

> *For the time will come when people will not tolerate sound doctrine, but, following their own desires, will surround themselves with teachers who tickle their ears. They will stop listening to the truth and will wander off to fables.*

Now, let's apply some of that to the messages being presented today.

CHAPTER 4

Questionable Aspects?

In early summer of 1986, I was privileged to be in Medjugorje. It was, perhaps, the last time anyone would see the area in its primitive state. Sixteen months later Fran and I returned to Medjugorje. The difference was startling. Commerce had come to the apparition site.

Interestingly, on that 1986 pilgrimage we had also traveled to Fatima for a few days. The area surrounding Fatima, of course, is one of commerce. Tourist shops, hotels, restaurants, etc. are everywhere. There are also a lot of extremely pious practices that have become common at both of those apparition sites. Some might call it sensationalism. Pilgrims (sometimes), and mostly locals, climb the apparition hills and mountains at Medjugorje barefoot. At Fatima, pilgrims walk to the site, some from very long distances, and they often do it barefoot. There is a special walkway at Fatima that covers the entire expanse of the shrine grounds and is used by pilgrims to approach the small center where the actual apparitions took place, by coming on their knees while they pray the Rosary. I thought it was something I should do, and found myself being photographed by countless people. I found out later that it was something women did there, but not men. Apparition sites have their own agendas and protocol.

At any rate, it is safe to also say that all apparition sites and similar locations of special religious fervor are overrun with commercialism and often are involved in certain aspects of sensationalism. However, with regard to the current activity in the Marian Movement in the United States, the sensationalism is a promotion and threatens to undermine the entire movement. Some examples follow.

Sensationalism

The headlines on promotional pieces are truly eye catching. One such piece states:

"He is Coming. Are You Prepared? Ann Ross Fitch (seer) clearly explains these sensational topics: Chastisement! The Three Days of Darkness! Secrets! God's Justice! End Times! The Second Coming of Jesus Christ!"

*   *   *   *

"Preparation for the Second Coming of Our Lord and Savior Jesus Christ," is the sub-heading on a book published from Scottsdale, Arizona. This two volume edition is basically composed of messages dealing with the chastisements.

*   *   *   *

"Tribulations and Triumph. Revelations on the Coming of The Glory of God," states a book headline from *Signs of the Times Magazine*. "Read and learn:
- Why the apparitions of Our Lady are about to close.
- The dangers that threaten the Pope and his place within Divine Providence.
- How the Antichrist is now alive—and plotting to fully exert his power in the world.
- How destruction will be unleashed on a scale never before witnessed in human history."

*   *   *   *

In many publications, there is a constant array of newly claimed messages that continue to promise all sorts of secret revelation, or material that apparently Jesus, the Bible, and the Church did not adequately explain. Messages about: The Great Apostasy. The Warning. The Miracle. World Economic Collapse. The Great Chastisement. The AntiChrist. The Comet and Fire from Heaven. The Three Days of Darkness.

*   *   *   *

New Video Release (promotion title)
"Biblical End Time Prophecies, by Br. Michael Dimond. If this video doesn't wake up people, nothing will. An explicit, hard-hitting exposé: The Mark of the Beast, an Insane Ruler of Russia, World War III and what people should do to prepare themselves for the days of tribulation."

*   *   *   *

Read about the messages concerning "fire falling from the sky." "Keep updated as the count down to God's justice begins." "Messages concerning the United States—And its collapse"—so states another promotion.

*   *   *   *

"The diabolical plans of this son of corruption (a Cardinal in the Vatican) slowly unfolds . . . the time for fulfillment is at hand . . . Today begins the rapid unfolding of the events to usher in the final holocaust of the end times. . . .

"The day of destruction is at hand . . . the Pope will die . . ." are parts of messages from another visionary as reported in a popular Marian Movement magazine.

*   *   *   *

The amount of material available today that concentrates on sensationalism (thus money) is becoming very frightening. It all hints secret revelation and chastisement along with proclaimed miracles. And why not; that is what many seem to be interested in. That's what seems to generate all the attention. That's what tweaks our curiosity, and even though the intentions might all be good, the results often times do not match the intentions. We are speaking here of the professional component in the Marian Movement, those who produce the books, the films, the newsletters (including me). In our zeal to promote this obvious age of Mary and supernatural manifestations, we are now prone to include anything that might spur interest or generate a following. That proclaimed miracle phase can include one or more of the following: Eucharistic miracles, weeping statues, icons or crucifixes, solar phenomena, and of course magic photos or healing waters.

Healing waters, or claims thereof, bring people. There are now many in the United States, and I am sure a number of them are what they claim to be. On the other hand . . .

Denise Morgan Estrada, in California, claimed she received messages that promised healings during the coming chastisement by mixing a brew made from the Hawthorn plant. (There was also a message whereby you would be saved if you wrote a special prayer on a piece of paper you were to keep with you, and when the chastisements came, you were to take this paper and swallow it).

In the Cleveland area, Maureen Sweeney announced a healing spring known as the "Maranatha Spring." The professional component of the Marian Movement may well be guilty of over-promoting these kinds of messages and giving undue rise to sensationalism. Such was the case with Denise Morgan's messages. With Maureen Sweeney, messages were published, supposedly from the Blessed Virgin Mary which included:

- "The abundance of grace that will flow from my spring will reveal **truths, heal, and bring peace . . .**" (emphasis in original).
- "Maranatha is the threshold of holy love and the gateway to the new Jerusalem."
- "The grace flowing from this spring will bring peace wherever it is taken."
- "The Triumph of My Immaculate Heart will begin today at Maranatha." (This was given on May 5, 1994.)
- "My heart opens to the world at this site. It is here that I will dispense every favor of my Motherly Heart."

It was stated that Our Lady would answer all needs here,

and that no one would be untouched. She stated that this
site was also her "blessing point" and stated: "I leave you
this sign of my presence amongst you. Press your rosaries
and other objects to it. Kiss it and venerate it. This is where
Heaven and earth have met. I promise many graces to those
who do so. Allow people to venerate it by kissing it. . . .
Please understand, any article you place here will carry
with it special grace to heal the infirm . . . and to take power
over darkness."

I would think there may be more than just a few who
would see "venerate it and kiss it" as bordering on idolatry.

A number of publications have taken to announcing sensational messages or supposed supernatural phenomena.
An example of this, used here to show the far reaching
affects it can sometimes cause, was the report of a weeping
statue of Our Lady at a small church (Salve Regina) in St.
Bernard, Ohio, as reported by a Bishop Athanasius Konstantinos, O.F.M. He supposedly is the Archbishop of the
"Orthodox Catholic Church of Russia in the Americas," as
reported by the publication that released this story.

St. Bernard, Ohio, is a community in the Cincinnati area
(as is my hometown of Milford), so it had a decidedly local
flavor. The claimed events had already started generating
the desired affect for the church of bishop Konstantinos.
Roman Catholics in this area went to Salve Regina Chapel to
view the weeping statue, AND, the Eucharistic miracle that
was now also claimed to have taken place. The chapel was
decorated to appeal to anyone who would claim to have a
"pre-Vatican II devotion," full of statues, icons, candles,
paintings, etc. The claims made by this church not only
lured many Catholics, it made a number of them believers,
and provided what all churches need to survive—money.

One report stated that Bishop Konstantinos, and a friend
named Brother Anthony, originally came to another
Cincinnati suburban church, St. George the Great, in 1992.
This church is a Russian Orthodox Church which
allegedly refused to accept the claim that he was an
ordained bishop, and the two finally accepted novice positions in a small monastery attached to the church. The
report had it that he left and eventually resurfaced as the
archbishop of this "Orthodox Catholic Church of Russia in

the Americas." I believe the Chancery of the Archdiocese of Cincinnati was aware of the existence of this church, and had stated in the diocesan paper several years ago that this was not a Catholic Church. However, they took no further position on the matter.

There was also a report that prior to this position in Cincinnati Bishop Konstantinos was a follower of a lady named Mary Ann Van Hoof in Wisconsin. This was the claimed seer in the Necedah, Wisconsin apparitions that were condemned by the Church some years ago. That would all be doubtful since Mary Ann Hoof has been deceased for probably 10 years. And all of this came from a claim as to a weeping statue. In any case, Archbishop Athanasius Konstantinos surfaced as the patriarch for the new church in Cincinnati.

To make matters worse, when the announcement was made by his church as to a weeping statue and a Eucharistic miracle, a man by the name of Andrew Wingate had also sent out a newsletter under the title of **Faithful and True of the Midwest**. The Faithful and True label belongs to groups who supported a claimed Australian visionary by the name of "The Little Pebble." This seer was responsible for all kinds of wild prophecy including one message that said he would be the next pope. Mr. Wingate was known as the seer, "Trumpeter of the Apocalypse" under the Little Pebble's format. Possibly because the Little Pebble couldn't ordain him, and seeing that the Little Pebble's empire was splintering, the Trumpeter of the Apocalypse was suddenly claiming to be a priest under Bishop Konstantinos at Salve Regina Church in St. Bernard. According to the "Trumpeter's" newsletter and the Faithful and True organization, he and Bishop Konstantinos were busy starting a new organization of priests under Our Lady's direction (another Marian Movement of Priests?), and who were to report directly to Pope John Paul II. (It was stated that this aspect of it was not yet actually in place.) The Trumpeter, now ordained, revealed he knew "all the details of the levels of hell, purgatory and heaven," and gave a full accounting of them. He said the bishop was busy bilocating around the world, setting up new churches and embarking on the final call "to unity."

Bishop Konstantinos claims that the "Tridentine Mass" is offered at Salve Regina Chapel. Further, he states: "We are only a poor Franciscan order." However, one needs to verify that Franciscan connection. (Father) Andrew Wingate, on the other hand, was busy formulating the "Marian Congress of Catholic Orthodox Bishops," claiming that over 20 bishops from three different rites had already joined this organization (several who were also visionaries). Pope John Paul II was evidently not yet aware that this was a new Catholic order, or that he was directly in charge of the new bishops conference. Bishop Konstantinos had been very active in signing up other small churches as his letterhead now includes the names of a number of other bishops and priests, and he even lists a number of various dioceses and regions that supposedly receive copies of his correspondence. The Trumpeter claimed he and the bishop had combined on fund raising projects, even setting up 900 numbers for this purpose.

On March 1, 1996, Bishop Athanasius Konstantinos sent out a very official letter, with proper stamps and seals, castigating the Faithful and True organization and Mr. Andrew Wingate, stating they were frauds. He stated he did not believe Mr. Wingate or Mr. William Kamm (The Little Pebble) were authentic, or in any way connected with Rome, and further, that he had to terminate all association with them. Finally, he stated that Mr. Wingate did not consecrate the miraculous host, but that one of his bishops in Mexico did. Considering the source it came from, all of that is amazing.

At the same time that all of the above was being discerned, another letter came to me from a lady in the southwest part of the United States telling a story about a friend of hers whose brother is a visionary, an orthodox priest, and who is known as the "Trumpeter of the Apocalypse." She sent details of a special medal that this Mr. (Rev.) Wingate was told to produce and wanted our opinion of it. Our opinion was similar to her pastor's who told her to trash it. The medal had a image of Mary standing atop the Trinity and the reverse side indicated that salvation comes through Mary.

There is no hard evidence here of an authentic Catholic Bishop. Mr. Wingate certainly isn't a Catholic priest. The church is not listed as Catholic and the weeping statue and the Eucharistic miracle is something we may want to stay away from. Interestingly, the Chancery of the Cincinnati Diocese seems to want nothing to do with all of these new developments and claims from Bishop Konstantinos. They seem to sense a legal limitation as to what you can and can't do regarding other peoples' beliefs and churches. And rightly so. But they sure could publish a notice for Roman Catholics advising them not to have anything to do with all of this if not proven true. Given the fact that the Cincinnati diocese is up to its eyeballs in some questionable visionaries and a "refuge community," it would seem like a positive step to try to get a handle on some of this.

But I think the real point here is that we can't just simply accept every claimed miracle no matter how much sensationalism is attached to it. And believe me, there is a lot of sensationalism being attached to everything being produced or published today.

Please recognize, that in the above example, this is THE EUCHARIST we're talking about here. And if it truly isn't a Eucharistic miracle, just how big of a blasphemy is that? What is our responsibility in checking these things out, and how guilty are we in participating if it is not true? What is the responsibility of the Archdiocese in matters involving the Eucharist, and in safeguarding the faith of its people?

Does sensationalism sell? Is it all real? Or just some of it? According to material produced in California, one seer provided a message that when the earthquake comes (she's been wrong three years in a row now), the valley of Santa Maria will be encased in a huge dome and people by the tens of thousands will come there for protection. Some already have.

But the biggest bit of sensationalism to hit in the past few years is the story that is going around right now. As I write this book (the end of May, 1996), the world awaits the great warning. This is the warning so many claimed visionaries have predicted, and which was part of the messages of Garabandal (which I think I believe in) thirty some years ago. This is the great warning that will occur just prior to the great signs to be left at a number of apparition sites, and which will usher in the purification of mankind. After a few false alarms and mis-fires by certain seers, this is to be the real thing, and this event will be witnessed by every man, woman, and child in the world. It is to happen by the end of May, 1996, as reported by different claimed visionaries—who shall not be named here.

In spite of all the letters, phone calls, faxs and newsletters that confirm the event, I do not believe in the time frame shown. That means that I am either going to look extremely foolish by the time this book hits the market, or some visionaries might. Maybe this book will have to be scrapped.

Then again, maybe you are now sitting there reading this and the world continues to struggle on, in spite of itself. Which was it?

Sensationalism? Medway, Massachusetts was touted as the Betania of North America and pulled people from as far away as Florida and California after the site for the new community (or refuge) was confirmed when Sr. Sims and Maria Esperanza located the property by finding a rock with Jesus' face on it.

"I hate to pass this information on," writes Fr. Heffernan, in his newsletter from Peterborough, Ontario, who then goes on to tell about some wild, cosmic occurrence that is about to happen because all the planets are lined up in a new formation, and etc. etc. Father Heffernan, God bless his vocation and his ministry, is often not shy about the chastisement/purification business, or about introducing visionaries.

We all know the state of the world today. We know that some very special things are happening. And our curiosity matches our concern for our soul and the souls of other family members. Sensationalism catches our eye very quickly, and it certainly sells books. But it is really very dangerous. I think we probably all admit to that already, in spite of ourselves.

Signs and Wonders

Jesus said we *would know the tree by its fruits*. Today, that is often interpreted to mean signs and wonders, and just as often, that is the only form of discernment being used. One critic of apparitions once told me that the only items for discerning apparitions being used today are a rosary and a camera. One is supposed to change color, and the other is supposed to produce a supernatural photo.

Still, this is a valid question: "What about all those signs? Don't they prove the authenticity of a visionary and apparition site?"

I think Jesus really answered that when he told us: "*Where two or three are gathered in my name, there am I in their midst*" (*Matt.* 18:20). If two or three are gathered . . .

How about two or three hundred? How about two or three thousand? How about 20,000?

Is your God so distant or disinterested in His people that He will not respond to thousands, after having said He would be there with just two or more?

Can't He respond to thousands of people who have gathered for all the right reasons; who have come at some cost and discomfort for His honor and glory; to receive His Sacraments; to pray and sing; to give honor and devotion to His Mother? Can't He turn to St. Peter and say: "Pete! Hit that number three switch and let's put on a little solar show for the good folks." Can't He recognize the presence of His people and provide a little confirmation that He has heard their request—in spite of who the claimed visionary is?

I think He can. Come to think of it, so can Satan. But, either way, that does not prove authenticity of a seer. Unfortunately, the signs and wonders have never been a major interest to the Church in discerning apparitions. That in no way is meant to disclaim the importance of signs and wonders. It is just that the Church recognizes the illusion aspect is more prevalent, as is Satan, and that physical healings and especially spiritual conversions are of much more importance.

Signs and wonders have always been with us. They are spoken of often in the Bible, including by Jesus Himself. He cautioned us to read the signs of the times and further told us that these things would be especially present to us in the last days. On the other hand, those "last days" have been going on for centuries it seems.

Regardless, angels, signs and wonders, miracles, and mystical phenomenon in the skies are simply facts we can't ignore. There are too many for at least some not to be authentic—just as with visionaries. But today, there seems to be too great an emphasis, plus a couple of new entries in the game. Today it is light shows, magic photos, angels, the "miracle of the sun" and rosaries turning gold.

Angels

Angels, of course, almost go without saying. Their existence is basic fundamental belief—not just Catholic belief, but most religious belief. Angels have become so "hot" in the past five years that they have rivaled the Blessed Virgin Mary in coverage. Unfortunately, much of this coverage has come from the **New Age Movement**. The number of books available on angels, emanating from New Age sources is wild, and angels are given credit for all kinds of things. The frightening aspect of that is that the same kind of credit is being given at countless apparition sites and by a seemingly endless list of people. Again, the need to discern is most important. In the New Age camp, there is no salvific mission of Jesus Christ, no Sacraments, no Mass, no Blessed Trinity, no Heaven or Hell. That is all you need to know to discern it.

On the other hand, "angel stories" go far beyond just New Agers or apparition sites. They have become prominent in many faiths, recounted on dozens of national TV shows, and in a whole stack of books. They have apparently been involved in all kinds of miraculous events and most cannot be disproven. They have also been involved in a truly remarkable number of events at apparition sites and have become commonplace at Medjugorje, for example.

Michael Brown, in a very comprehensive book on this subject, *The Trumpet of Gabriel*, goes into the subject in great depth. He shows both sides. That certain "false angel of light" can, and does come with sweets for those with a sweet tooth.

Rosaries, The Sun, And Light Shows

About six or seven years ago there was a particularly large amount of controversy regarding rosaries "turning gold" (color). A number of scientific—and not so scientific—explanations were presented for this claimed phenomena. One of the more prevalent was that it was simply the result of low grade metal and what happens to it over the years. I guess, sort of like your silver teapot tarnishing.

I recall at that time we asked a friend who was going to

Medjugorje on pilgrimage, to take a box of new white chain rosaries, and a box of black ones, to be blessed by the priests there, and if possible, to have them blessed in the apparition room. The rosaries had never been used, and in fact, were still sealed in plastic . . . probably about four dozen in all.

When the rosaries came back to us I simply shoved them in a drawer to fill future requests for a "rosary blessed at Medjugorje." When I had to fill such a request, I was astonished to see that both bags (still sealed) now contained golden chain rosaries. All the others in the drawer still had their silver color.

The miracle of the sun phenomena? I have witnessed it in Medjugorje. But moreover, I have witnessed it twice in Milford, Ohio—once standing in my driveway. It was a Saturday morning and Fran and I had just returned home from morning Mass. I was having a tough time. We were way over-worked, I had a very important book (*Messages and Teachings of Mary in Medjugorje*) in French that needed translating, and we had no translator. I remember, while picking up the morning paper on the driveway, specifically asking the Lord if He knew what He was doing up there, and "how about a little help."

As I straightened back up, for some reason I glanced up at the sun—and there it was, pounding away. I quickly told the Lord, "never mind," and decided it would all work out. But the solar phenomenon was getting to be commonplace. It was the miracles that happened the next two days that really confirmed God's actions, and His presence to me.

Light shows are even more spectacular—and controversial. Obviously they are usually seen at night, or when natural light is such that it allows this type of activity to be seen. Flashing and sparkling lights everywhere!

Since most visionaries claim that Our Lady always comes proceeded by brilliant light (and rightly so, I would think), this kind of activity is, perhaps, to be expected. If you have enough people who claim to witness these events, how are you going to prove they don't exist. Locally (Cincinnati and Northern Kentucky), this type of activity was claimed to have been witnessed by many, including several priests, when Mary was allegedly appearing here. There are also numerous claims of conversions, and people equate their return to the Church and to the Sacraments based on witnessing these manifestations.

What about all of this phenomena? Isn't that proof? It may well be. Then again, maybe not! Doesn't the name "Lucifer" indicate an angel of light? Doesn't it say in the Bible that he can and will come as a false angel of light? Christine Gallagher is a highly touted visionary from Ireland. She also claims many experiences and battles with Satan and states that the "greatest light shows" she has seen have been put on by the devil. If Satan has such incredible powers to deceive and to destroy, to work miracles, to even take the Lord to the top of a mountain where he showed Him all the kingdoms of the world, can he turn the color of a rosary chain? If he can come as the Blessed Virgin Mary or the Lord (attested to by many of the saints), can he create solar phenomena or a light show? St. Catherine had visions and apparitions for many years. Feeling herself favored with great graces, she had said audaciously to the devil: "Know that you could send me no temptation without my perceiving it." After this imprudent challenge, she had false apparitions of Our lord and Our Lady for five years (from "*Revelations: How to Judge Them*," page 371).

There have been spectacular light shows at Bayside for years. Also at Necedah, Wisconsin. The sun performed dances there as well. Rosaries turned gold. An aunt of Fran's once showed me a rosary that turned golden color, on the spot, in Necedah. She doesn't believe in the claimed apparitions there, but did attest as to what happened to her there. Signs and wonders have always been prevelant at false apparition sites. Are we to believe that Satan is so inept that he cannot perform "miracles" as well?

There are two points to keep in mind.
1) The Church puts very little credence in mere signs and wonders in judging claimed apparitions, and,
2) Satan can and does perform some of his own.

But perhaps the biggest rouse of all, and the most common phenomena to devotees of apparition sites today is the photograph. Like everything else connected with mysticism, some are undoubtedly authentic. And many are not.

Magic Photos

The number of photos currently being passed around, the world over, is frightening. We have seen one picture which is claimed to have come from four different apparition sites as being "an authentic picture taken by so-and-so at such-and-such place." The quality of the picture gets worse and worse the more it travels and the more copies and reproductions are made. One popular photo of Mary and the baby Jesus was traced to the cover of a German Christmas card. Another popular photo had been initially shown to me on my first trip to Medjugorje by our spiritual director, Fr. Ken Roberts. He stated that the photo was originally taken by a priest while traveling through the desert out west. It shows the Virgin Mary interwoven into a shrub or bush that the priest was especially attracted to along the side of the highway. The photo then resurfaced all over the world as a miraculous photo originating from various apparition sites.

Polaroid photos are the most popular and convey all kinds of images, particularly if taken into the sun or a strong light. All kinds of images can appear. What most people seem to be getting today is an image of "the doorway to Heaven." Some of the images are impressive. Some really take a lot of imagination to see what someone else is claiming to see.

The same is true of video cameras. Some produced startling results. Some are questionable. On the local scene, an analysis of a video tape as conducted by Xavier University and by the WKRC Television station, regarding light and solar phenomena at a claimed apparition site, did not come up with very good results.

Though some of the photos I have seen are truly remarkable, most are not, and some almost absurd. If you find yourself looking at a bunch of squiggly lines that are supposedly dancing lights on an otherwise black photo, you might want to question it . . . or if you have to tax your imagination to just figure out what you're supposed to be looking at. Like many other articles associated with apparitions or sites, pictures quickly find their way to the marketplace. More than one firm has made the distribution of these photos its special objective. Regardless, the Church will *NEVER* approve

or authenticate any apparition based on photos, but it may
be the reason to condemn some.

Perhaps it is worth taking the time and space here to further analyze two photos that are particularly popular—and
troublesome. One is a photo of a weeping John Paul II super-
imposed in the arms of the Blessed Virgin Mary. *A Call to
Peace* newsletter reported that the photo originated with a
group of pilgrims from Amsterdam who took some photos
while on pilgrimage and etc. etc., and ultimately this photo
was the result when all the negatives were finally developed, enlarged, etc. etc.

In 1993, the magazine, *Echo of Medjugorje*, stated: "The
picture of the Pope in Our Lady's arms is not a miraculous
photo come out of who knows whose camera. It is a painting from Cracow in Poland."

An even more controversial and popular photo is known
as "the true image of Jesus." And, maybe it is. Why can't it
just be a painting by some artist? This portrait of the head
and shoulders of Our Lord, incredibly, is supposed to be not
only the true image of Jesus, but He is supposed to be truly
present in the picture. A letter by Father Jose Aleson, dated
May 7, 1991, details this claim. He quotes a visionary from
Spain who speaks for Jesus.

In part, the letter states: "I reside there, alive, My presence
is there." The letter goes on to say that "several times our
Lord has made statements about such pictures and the miracles produced, about how when He returns triumphant we
shall witness Him coming out of the picture itself and out of
the Holy Eucharist. He said to pray a lot in front of His picture. His eyes will see the good and bad we do. He said not
to laminate it, and we should not enclose it in glass as in a
picture . . ."

Cyndi Cain and her newsletter, *A Call to Peace*, was a leading promoter of this photo. Her newsletter took up the
defense by printing an article by a Rev. Venard-Marie
Poslusney who defended Fr. Aleson and had the photo
affirmed by visionaries and locutionists from all over (most
of whom are themselves questionable). Fr. Poslusney stated
he was present in Palestine when the original pictures were
taken from whence this miraculous image came. Fr. Robert
Burns, in Nebraska, also defended the photo.

A number of investigations have been made regarding this photo and the results are certainly not in favor. One such report came from the newsletter/magazine, *Catholic Commentary*. They reported that "it seems as though the original image was painted in Europe, and is hanging in a museum in Italy. Prints of the original were made . . . One such old print may be found in the 'Stone House' located on the Cabrini Shrine property just outside Denver, Colorado. Others are being reported as hanging in certain churches, in homes, or in storage."

Wouldn't it simply suffice to say "here is a nice painting of Jesus" than to line up claimed visionaries who endorse it—or reject it?

The "End Times Apostles" in Colorado have also issued a strong rebuke of the picture as being a false claim. They offer some compelling arguments. Additionally, the "true presence" of Jesus now seems to be available for a price. A number of ministries have hopped on this bandwagon and offer the true image of Jesus in all sorts of sizes and price ranges. An example would be "The Lady of the Apocalypse" ministry, in Westminster California. The claims and promotions related to this photo are in need of urgent investigation by the Church.

I believe there is only one true image of Jesus, and there is only one, truly certain place of His presence. It is called a tabernacle. That is where He is. And His true image is a host. It is the Eucharist that He Himself established and makes available to us every single day. He has never asked us to worship and adore photos. He never told us He would return someday by coming out of some photo, or statue, or maybe just come down off of crucifixes.

In a time when His "True Presence" is being doubted by many in the Church, when we struggle to re-establish devotion to the Blessed Sacrament, is it acceptable to support this kind of promotion? You no longer need the Blessed Sacrament or the Monstrance. All you need is a photocopy machine. Push a button and pump out another 50 "truly present Jesus' in photo form."

Who needs a Mass and the Consecration? Who needs a priest? You have the real thing right here in this picture. And all for only $2.00—or $22.00.

Yes, undeniable things are happening. A merciful God is calling to His People and conversions and renewal abound. So does the spiritual warfare. The Bible tells us to keep oil in our lamps and keep them lit for *"Satan is prowling about the world like a lion ready to devour souls."* Test everything! Discern! Don't believe every single claim that somebody throws at you just because it involves Jesus or Mary.

Your rosary turning gold, or a photo, will never prove an apparition, or authenticate a visionary. Neither will a light you see, unless you can truly verify whose light it is.

Money

"So, we plead with you to help Our Blessed Virgin Mary to spread out **FAST** these Most Urgent Messages, and also to send us a good donation of **$25 or more** . . ." (emphasis in the original). So read the flyer from the "Mission of the Blessed Virgin Ministry" in Westminster, California. The messages being distributed there come from an alleged visionary named Sister Guadalupe.

Requests for financial support have sort of been synonymous with religion. It's nothing new. It's ingrained in us. There is a need to economically support the various foundations of our faith, and our houses of worship and education centers. But we also need to recognize another reality here and that is that supernatural phenomena has become big business. Apparitions of the Blessed Virgin Mary (and Jesus and angels as well) have become an industry. Sadly, some efforts supposedly aimed at our salvation have turned into quests for big bucks.

Let's don't even get started on the premise that everyone involved in this business is only out for money. That is obviously not true—no more so than characterizing every false visionary as diabolical.

There are, indeed, some wonderful people responding to the evangelization call these days who ardently believe in what they are doing but who are being deluded somewhere along the way. Some simply don't have the capabilities to financially participate in doing "the Lord's work" that they think they are doing. And then again, some probably know exactly what they are doing—and why.

It's not too difficult to assess the motives behind the sud-

den influx of TV shows dealing with supernatural manifestations. They go with what is hot, with where the profit is,
with where the ratings are. Fame, fortune, and controlling
public motivation and interest is where it is at. That is all
the more obvious when, in watching any of those programs,
you find they lump Nostradamus, Edgar Cayce and
UFOlogy together with angels and the Blessed Virgin Mary.
To them, all the New Age flap-trap is the same as Fatima in
content (and so is the $$).

Those of us who publish and distribute materials
involved with this wild and exciting "Marian Age," and
those of you who are the subscribers and the end users of
this material must strive not to be that naive, or that com-
mercially motivated.

> "As many of you know, a life devoted to full-
> time ministry is very expensive. Thanks be to God
> for those who so generously support us so that we
> can continue to minister full-time. The Lord says,
> **'Ask and you shall receive,'** and so we are asking
> your help . . ."

So states a solicitation flyer from a purported visionary in
Arizona. An Apostolate in Pennsylvania suggests you tithe
and send $5.00 a month. They also suggest you finance their
new building. Solicitations and requests for money are now
commonplace for organizations involved in the "business
end" of the Marian Movement.

Well, balderdash!

A full-time ministry does **not** have to be "very expensive."
Nor are you expected to have to finance everyone else's
efforts. Nor has Our Lady asked you to. Nor does every sup-
posed "good work" need your monetary blessing if it is, in
fact, being done solely for the honor and glory of God. You
have a right (read "responsibility") to question all of these
requests for funds, and especially so if they come sur-
rounded by sensational claims and promises.

Before looking at some examples of the money issue in
some of the efforts of the professionals in the "apparition
industry," we should first mention that those same efforts
have produced incredibly positive results as well. Con-

sider how many people (souls) have been reached by the
promotions of all of these books and videos on apparitions
and messages? They ignited an interest. How many people
have been reached by TV programs that also sparked an
interest, or by authors or publishers participating in radio
call-in shows that generate renewed interest in God and
the plight of the world? The secular media, dastardly
though it may be, has aided the effort as well, simply
because they can't explain all of this either. Not everyone
has their hand out, nor is every publisher (including this
one) also having visions—of dollar signs only. But there
is also plenty of evidence to show that the promotion end
of all of this is somewhat out of control as is the visionary/
locutionist end of it.

Along with the promotion for the "final dogma" of Mary,
one publisher then produced a story dealing with the fact
that the Miraculous Medal—which has been around for centuries—is suddenly not correct. This most respected sacramental, acknowledged by the Church for so long, is
suddenly in need of replacement, based upon a claimed
visionary who confirms that St. Catherine's advisors and
directors did not produce the medal according to Our Lady's
wishes. Interestingly, some of the same people that promote
the dogma, and unity, and the new revelations about the
error with St. Catherine, are the same people who are promoting a new and correct medal. You can now get a Virgin
of the Globe Medal, in 14K gold, for a mere $225. Sterling
silver, $30.

A lady in California is supplying special painted images
of Our Lady, and "earth" rosaries for only $65.00 each. The
problem is, she is up to her ears in all kinds of New Age
imagery. T-shirts, coffee mugs, pins, pendants, angel or
Mary wrist-watches—you can purchase every conceivable
religious item through the mail from Marian Promoters.
And I guess that's fine. But then why should you be
expected to also donate funds to organizations that are selling materials. Statues for thousands of dollars? I wonder if
Our Lady would rather see you donate that money to one of
the new orphanages in Croatia or Bosnia where a whole
bunch of kids no longer have any fathers . . . or homes . . .
or shoes . . . or in some cases, even feet? I wonder if she

would rather you spend the $50.00 on medical supplies for handicapped war refugees instead of a gold-filled, 12K, engraved Two Hearts medal?

You have a right to question it. And especially, question every request for money that comes to you as somebody's "request from Mary, or from Jesus," or that even hints that you are letting Our Lady down if you don't help financially to get her messages out. If Our Lady, or Her Son, really want a book distributed, or some devotion to spread, do you really think they are incapable of pulling it off without your help?

I know from our own experience, we have produced a number of "not for profit" books, books in the $2.00 range, that we run no ads for, no promotional flyers—we can't afford to—and yet these books get reprinted dozens of times and the distribution reaches into the hundreds of thousands. Why is that? How can that happen?

Why do we think we always have to be more clever than the Lord? **Let God be God!**

One of the more notable success stories concerning the distribution of materials involving apparitions, messages, prophecies and locutionists is the **Signs of the Times** organization. Ted and Maureen Flynn have put material into the hands of many thousands of people. The book, *The Thunder of Justice*, is a great success story unto itself. But as apparitions and the number of claimed visionaries grow more and more out of control, we have to ask whether some of these kinds of materials are falling into the same trap. So many today are now totally steeped in sensationalism and the quest and call for money. They get hawked and promoted like T-shirts and bumper stickers at the site of some disaster. As example, a multi-page flyer produced on the above book listed recommendations for it and one included Fr. Paul Marx, President of **Human Life International**, who stated:

"Great. I'll take 1,000!"

In the case of the above book, HLI could order the 1,000 copies to give away free in return for a donation of $30.00 or more. In doing so, they stated that "this amazing book sells for $18 at retail, but it's yours free . . ."

There is also a right, and a need to question any distributor of materials who is offering those materials for a price, and who, at the same time is seeking our donations.

Of course we need money. All of us. And most certainly those whose efforts are being offered in the Lord's behalf. We cannot afford **NOT** to support ministries who labor in a secular and materialistic world for the salvation of souls. It is our obligation. But part of that obligation is to also make sure what you are donating for, and to whom, and where it is going. It is what this book is about, this thing called discernment, and the fact that Satan is never going to be content to merely sit on the sidelines while we are doing all these good works, without trying to mess it all up. He can turn our heads and our hearts; he can cloud our vision and our mental capacities. He can finish by having good people, well intentioned in their goals, objectives and efforts, tarnish those goals, objectives and efforts by turning them into secularistic and economic ventures.

Is this really happening or has Bill Reck gone off the deep end? Is this just adding more confusion to the whole thing, or condemning everyone else's motives or actions? I don't think so. The confusion is already out there—everywhere. It can best be shown by using examples that are items already known or that have already occurred.

One publishing firm is headed by a priest who had formerly stated he was the spiritual advisor to Vassula Ryden. He became involved with two other claimed visionaries following a pilgrimage to Europe and published books on their messages and experiences. He stated that **he** was approving these messages, that the seers were instructed by Our Lady to have these books published (as always), and added that "the book is destined to be a world's Best Seller in many languages." The promotional flyer goes on to say "news releases, feature stories, flyers/posters (adapted to your business) are available, as well as speakers for talks, conferences, guest appearances."

Six or seven years ago, there were several major Marian Conferences held across the United States. The first was the result of the efforts of Denis Nolan and his fine group at South Bend, Indiana, and held at Notre Dame. There were nine thousand of us who attended. Today there are twenty to thirty such Marian Conferences. For all the good accomplished, for all the spiritual conversions and the good fruits that have come from them, in some ways they have regressed—no doubt under the efforts of you-know-who. There are indications of discontent, competition, jealousy from one site to another, a clamor to get more "visionaries" as speakers than another conference had, and so on. But there has also been an additional change, and it is called profit. Some locations found out that not only could they finance their ministry and the promotion of the conference through the operation of a "bookstore" there, but that they could make a profit as well. In some cases it has simply been approached with the specifications of a secular convention:

> Table fee for exhibitor: $125.00
> Commission to conference: 25% of gross sales
> Exhibitor responsible for shipping
> Handling charge: first 110 pounds free. Additional: $24.00 per 100 lbs.

In the past couple of years, the concept of the "Marian Conference" took on a new dimension in that the event became a Caribbean Cruise. Many visionaries—believing their humility was not at issue, I guess—were happy to participate and speak to the captive audience. From the materialistic standpoint, one couldn't complain about the dollars spent though, since more is spent going to Medjugorje or Betania or San Nicolás.

Some apostolates seem to have been simply caught up in a never ending appeal for money to stay alive. It is necessary to refer to a ministry operating in the northeast states as an example here. This ministry is involved with the publishing of new devotional materials, a new medal, a booklet pertaining thereto, and other materials. It was an offshoot of the original goal of the ministry which was to promote Our Lady of Guadalupe. There is a very heavy solicitation for funds from this ministry, even including transferring your long distance telephone service to an organization known as LifeLine, who is then going to give 10% of that long distance billing to this apostolate. I believe the "Catholic League for Religious and Civil Rights" have had some doubts about the LifeLine operations.

With respect to the above example, some expressed concern with the claimed visionaries and the devotional material itself, to begin with.

Though it is stated that the request for the new booklet

and medal is so great that it all has to be reprinted again, "the apostolate does not have the funds necessary to print the booklets . . ." According to the reports of others, however, there were enough funds to hire two professional fund raisers at substantial salaries, and pay a substantial salary and all expenses to the president of the ministry. Four-page brochures are mailed out in large quantities seeking donations, usually with the standard offering of a free book in return for a donation of $_____ or more.

Everyone has the right to question all of these solicitations for money, from me or anyone else. And in repeating that, we also need to state that this can be extremely difficult at times. In fund raising—and I'm not just talking about professionals in the Marian Movement here, but all fund raising efforts—you have to realize that these are sometimes very professional and skilled people who head up these efforts, and those efforts are going to include whatever can reach your heart before it tries to reach your checkbook.

Please continue to give to the many worthwhile and needy organizations for they deserve our support. But it is time to really start discerning what is happening in the Marian Movement today, and that concerns not only visionaries, but money as well. The Holy Spirit speaks to you—to each of us. Just as you should put down that latest or newest message book from wherever because you are very uncomfortable with it, so you should not support any request for funds that makes you feel the same way. The *"Sensus Fidelium"* has a history of usually being correct, whenever they practice discernment. If you can't resolve the issue yourself, seek some assistance before you jump in.

Aside from the professional element in the Marian Movement activity today, what about the visionaries/locutionists themselves?

I think we all need to be totally honest with each other here. When you have as many new visionaries, locutionists, devotional materials, message books and claimed apparition sites popping up as we have today, you know money can become a major concern with at least a portion of it.

There are some visionaries, past and present, that stand out as special role models for us. Almost all of the saints and seers of the past were noted for their humble lifestyles and the fact that they were so seldom in the limelight. Today, Sr. Lucia, the visionary from Fatima is a prime example. Given the proven historical accuracy of Fatima and the fact that Lucy is the only survivor, she could be quite a celebrity in her own right. Instead, look what she has chosen. She lives in a cloistered convent. How about Mother Teresa?

In spite of what the critics might claim, the visionaries of Medjugorje are also prime examples. If these events were not authentic, do you really think that you would stay with it this long if you were one of the seers involved. There have been countless opportunities to bail out. Consider the fact that they have not written books (as most claimed American visionaries), produced films, accepted small fortunes from over-zealous followers, or moved to other glamorous parts of the world (Marija lives part time in Italy). In spite of great devastation and war, and in spite of economic hardship, they are still clinging to the same beliefs. They have been consistent; their spirituality has remained intact, and money has not become their idol. Do they make a living? Certainly, the same as all of us must do. But there is not a whole lot of profit or glamour living in a ravaged and economically depressed region, especially when your enemies are also opposed to your religious convictions. God bless them for their convictions and faith.

Unfortunately, we can't always say that about many other claimed visionaries. One of the major items in the criteria for judging private revelation by the Church is: "Who is economically benefitting from this? Who is making money off of it?" That seems to be an area of discernment that we seem to skip over today. Another area is pride versus humility. As noted above there are some pretty strong role models of this century that we can use as a standard for evaluating the humility of a visionary versus the pride and ego we are all subject to. In some aspects, it is not possible to separate the money part from the pride.

There are forty to fifty message books available for us to read, all published during the past eight years from American seers/locutionists. (A few I myself published). In many cases, these books have been published because the Blessed Virgin Mary or Jesus has personally requested it. That is doubtful. Pride and ego come into the discernment picture as the mystic becomes more involved in speaking engagements, conferences, retreats, book signings, and travelling around the country, if not the world. It can be a consuming pattern. So can money.

Is a visionary being paid a royalty on the publication of these books? Is there a lot of profit involved? (Profit is NOT a sin, or a dirty word). If so, who is getting it? What economic gain has taken place because of the publishing of some book on private revelation, and who received it?

This may be a good place to answer some questions which may be on the minds of many readers—and rightly so—regarding the author of this book.

Have I ever paid a royalty to a visionary on a book? Yes I have. It is something I will very heavily discern in the future, and probably will never do again. I did it only once, and I'm not sure if it actually didn't do the person involved more harm than good, even economically.

Have I ever personally benefitted from the publishing of such a book? No, I don't think so.

Have profit margins for such books been excessive in our case? Interestingly, the most profit we have received from books dealing with private revelation have been those books where we priced them not to make a profit. To me, that only proves that Jesus is much smarter than I am. Let God be God.

Have I ever been deceived in the area of private revelations and the traps that lurk about in the form of money, pride, or false messages? You bet! Through only the grace of God, I think we caught and corrected them in the process.

It is tough. It is very deceptive. Bad private revelation is a kiss of death to the great gifts and charisms that our Lord God is making available to us in so many ways today. You are doing yourself, your Church, the claimed visionary involved, and the entire Marian Movement a great good by questioning these things, and discerning these points with every new book or claimed apparition anyone (including me) presents to you.

How many Scriptural quotations could we include here regarding pride, ego, money, status, fame, publicity, wealth, power? How many words of Jesus could we quote? How many examples could be presented to show the pitfalls, and the results, of the above traits? Do we start with Judas selling Jesus for thirty pieces of silver? Why do we need to start at all? This is a topic, an issue, that I am asking the reader to answer. This is an issue I wish for you to discern on your own. Come up with your own standards. And when you do, then apply those examples and standards against the never ending supply of new books and materials you are receiving every week on new revelation being provided by so many visionaries, well intentioned though they be. That "right" to question economic gain and personal success can even be looked upon as an obligation.

It is **not** being judgmental. Judging is part of that process we have been sorely lacking, and it is known as **discernment**.

A claimed visionary in the Cincinnati area is personally involved in displaying, promoting and distributing her own message books to Churches, prayer cenacles, liturgies, Marian Centers, etc. That is not presented as some condemnation of someone, but is being used as an example. Unfortunately, it is being repeated by a number of claimed visionaries around the United States.

Does the area of economic gain, and pride and ego become a big factor here? And what if it involves a seer not openly endorsed by the Church? Or a book that is highly questionable? Is fame and ego a major driving force?

We all need to return to one, simple, basic fact. This is only private revelation. It involves a mere human being just like the rest of us. It cannot add to revelation, nor is it offered by someone infallible. It may or may not be credible. There is not one single visionary—or all of them put together—who should command your veneration, or even your acceptance, based only on their claimed gifts.

It seems most new material being produced today, regarding private revelation, does not include any attempt to obtain Church approval in the form of an *Imprimatur*. In fact, most shy away from it recognizing questionable messages are involved, or even some material that was changed to make it more acceptable to the reader. On the other hand, there are often attempts by the same producers to obtain Church approvals and *Imprimaturs* for certain prayers, meditations, chaplets, etc. from the same visionary in order to make it appear the Church has formally accepted her or him.

We all need to realize as well that this supposed license to publish anything and everything, by simply sticking some disclaimer on the copyright page of a book quoting the removal of a couple of Canons from the *Code of Canon Law* dealing with private revelation, may be a hidden curse. You, as the reader of these materials, have no obligation whatsoever to support or accept these materials based solely on the personal theology being presented by the publisher or author on how and why Our Lord wants you to do such and such. You have no obligation whatsoever regarding private revelation except the obligation to discern everything any producer or publisher is presenting to you—including me.

Mix And Match

It is a real roller coast ride sometimes, trying to make sense out of all of this supernatural business. It goes from being chaotic, to humorous, to tragic, to outright confusion. Along come new beliefs, new theories, and of course, new sets of prophets (somehow, today we have come up with this highly questionable term of "voiceboxes").

In this century we seem to have more than just a few new twists and turns, ups and downs. Along with dissension within the Church, we've become involved in secular humanism, a return to the occult, Communism, all kinds of new forms of old pagan rites, and the culmination of it all in this proclaimed panacea, **The New Age Movement**.

In the New Age concept, hot topics like angels and visitations from Jesus and Mary are finely intertwined so as to fit in with everybody's beliefs. The result is sort of a mix-and-match offering of available supernatural goodies for your enjoyment and use. The New Age and the Occult (they are closely aligned) are at the root of much of it. We say "much" because there is also a growing number of just plain hucksters in the Jesus/Mary/Angel business who aren't interested in any of the three, or in Satan, but just simply see a great opportunity to make some really nice $$$. But most of it seems to have strings attached, and those strings ultimately lead back to he who we do not wish to be associated with.

Right off the bat, the word **discernment** rears its head here. Who is to say Jesus or Mary can't appear to a New-Ager, or to an outright pagan? Wasn't there a Paul who used to be known as Saul who persecuted Christians until somebody knocked him off of a horse? And how do we know there isn't some conversion involved here? Well, we probably don't. But you can go pretty far with discernment pretty fast, just with studying the messages a little bit. Don't just read them, but study them.

Harper-Collins Publishers, one of the nation's largest, issued a news release in 1995 announcing a new book titled, *Gifts of Grace*. It is listed as "a gathering of personal encounters with the Virgin Mary." An image of Our Lady adorns the cover, and the context of the promotional piece is well written and alludes to all the factors we would want to see in such a book—grace, conversion, healings, peace, and the existence of a Supreme Being, as well as a supernatural mother. But if you keep reading, she becomes a "universal mother," and with the suggestion that the "Virgin Mary is a manifestation of Mother Earth. She is a figure of amazing feminine energy . . . Madame Pele, the Hawaiian goddess of fire; she is the White Buffalo Calf Woman; and the Crystal Woman. Mary tells us they are all one. We are the Mother energy of all that is."

I recently received a letter from a "cloistered" in California that spoke highly of healings and the scent of roses. It said "the new Living Rosary is sung here daily." The letter was an inquiry about our willingness to publish material they wanted to distribute. But the material spoke of: "our covenant with the higher self; interludes of bliss with the spheres and the gifts of Shekinah . . . a call to align with Mother in the highest etheric realms . . . Bring forth 'the Radiance Light' of all inner energy chakras." It referred to the "Temple of Creative Healing Wisdom" and named Mary as the Divine Light.

The above material is all associated with a religion known as **The New Age Movement (NAM)**. And it indeed is a religion. It seldom comes in the form of a religion, but more in the form of new self-awareness, seeking our higher self, reaching our state of connection with a higher realm. It has taken full advantage of the fact that Mary and angels are hot topics.

Angels! Angel books are everywhere. *Embraced by the Light* became a national best seller (though now heavily critiqued as being highly questionable at best). TV programs gave primetime coverage to all sorts of "near death experiences," and unexplainable happenings. The supernatural has become a catch-all phrase to include the occult, the New Age, angels and Mary, UFOlogy, and untold "mystics" who grace the television late-night airwaves with all of those "900 numbers" you can call to get a handle on your future. Don't doubt for a minute there are spirits involved in all of this. Don't doubt for a minute as to just what kind of spirits they are, either. Or who sent them.

Publishers and merchandisers of NAM materials have capitalized enormously on the angel phenomena. For example, a lady named Terry Lynn Taylor (California) produces a newsletter titled *"Angels Can Fly."* It is a well done and very informative publication that quotes liberally from the Bible and gives credence not only to angels but to a number of saints as well. You can even order angel or Mary holy cards, and a Miraculous medal. On the other hand, Taylor also liberally quotes from other New Age sources and authors (Corrine Heline for example) and sprinkles in Buddhism and quotes from Zen masters. Mother earth is prominent, as well as plants and flowers. Taylor co-ordinated a conference in New Mexico, in 1993, titled "Angels and Nature Spirits Conference" which included a whole line-up of New Age speakers and advocates.

Books dealing with the Blessed Virgin Mary often border on the bizarre and include wild combinations of Christian and other Catholic beliefs with some of the more far left New Age beliefs. The aforementioned Corrine Heline was one of the first in this scenario authoring a book titled *The Life and Mission of the Blessed Virgin*. She also produced a New Age interpretation of the Bible and a book titled *Tarot and the Bible*, among others.

Peggy Tabor Mullin, through Celestial Arts Company, a New Age publishing house in Berkley, California, wrote *Mary's Way*. It includes a pilgrimage to Medjugorje which she claims changed her life forever. However, she then ties it into her studies in metaphysics, attitudinal healing, and Siddha Yoga. She relates experiences in Medjugorje to crystals, mandalas, and the Sanskirt Om and defined the Croatian Mass as "mesmerizing, like a mantra that takes one immediately to that inner room."

One of the most recognized New Age books dealing with supposed messages from the Blessed Virgin Mary is *Mary's Messages to the World*, authored by Annie Kirkwood. It is almost unimaginable that any Christian, much less any Catholic could take this book seriously as it offends many Christians and Catholic beliefs.

Annie Kirkwood reports that Mary has told her that: She and Joseph had many other lives . . . Joseph once lived as a nun and she was once a faith healer in India . . . Other planets have been prepared for our arrival after the earth splits and turns on its side . . . UFOs will be seen almost daily—visitors from other planets . . . There will be two suns . . . It doesn't matter what religion you belong to . . . She and Joseph had eight children . . . One day you will be able to travel on love . . . The terms "salvation" and "power of the Cross" are fictitious and there is no place known as Heaven . . . Put aside the Bible and go to the altar of your mind . . . You have all lived for eons, first in one body, then in another.

If all that isn't enough, Jesus then comes on the scene to verify reincarnation, "automatic writing," "channeling," and explains that the woman in the book of Revelation is "mother earth" and that Satan does not exist.

Quantum Conceptions, in Bellingham, Washington, produces a program titled "Shekinah Grace Teachings" under the direction of a channeler named Christina Marie Stephans. Stephans incorporates all Church approved apparitions—such as Lourdes and Fatima—into her brochure. This program, New Age throughout, further identifies our "divine Mother" as also being the Holy Spirit.

Another book to emerge, much more Catholic in content by first impression, comes from Three Eras Inc. The book is titled *The Book of the True Life*, and includes, apparently, twelve volumes. The teachings therein, from "the Divine Master," were supposedly channeled through a mystic in Mexico who was used as Elijah the Prophet.

SOURCE, from Hornbrook, California, produces a booklet called *Mary's Sun Letters*. The publisher is Mary Clarice McChrist, director of an organization known as "The Mother Matrix." In the book, Mary calls us to call upon her Son, Lord Jesus, and to ask for her help. She says she comes with messages of hope and urges us to pray the Rosary. She speaks of her Immaculate Heart and asks us to dedicate ourselves to it.

With all of that said, the book also states Mary has been given the new title of "Lord Mary Buddha." She apparently calls us to a new awakening, to our own divinity, and we should prepare by going to bodyworkers for energetic healing. She redefines one of her titles as "The Immaculate Concept," and gives instruction on how to ground yourself with mother earth.

Not unexpectedly, much of the material promoting the NAM comes from California and Arizona. Sedona, Arizona, is a hotbed of New Age and early Indian beliefs. A magazine titled *Sedona: Journal of Emergence* is published there. One of many such publications, it is a compilation of articles provided by healers, psychics, channelers and New Age authors, and ads for just about anything available under the NAM umbrella.

Please be aware that much of this material is being utilized in the Catholic Church today. It is principally centered in retreat houses, but also in convents, seminaries, and universities.

I recently came across a magazine article titled: "Virgin Mary manifestations in Florida." It stated that thousands of people are flocking to a modest Florida house to "hear a woman deliver messages from the Virgin Mary. Rosa Lopez says that she receives daily messages from the Virgin who urges more prayer and devotion."

The articles goes on to report that all the right things are supposedly happening there. There is water flowing out of a fountain beneath a statue of Mary in Rosa's front yard and there are signs and wonders—claimed healings. We have one major problem here. This article appeared in the most recognized New Age and Occultic magazine in the United States (and known worldwide) titled *Share International*. It is tied in to the Tara Center—a New Age and occult organization in California—affiliated with the Satanic *Lucis Trust,* and produced by a gentleman by the name of Benjamen Creme who is the point man for the supposed antichrist, who goes under the name of Lord Maitreya. He, it is reported, is living in London.

Listen to what the Holy Spirit is whispering within your heart and mind. Don't take everything at face value out of concern for not pleasing the Mother of Jesus. Instead, try to spend a little effort to first decide if it is really coming from the Mother of Jesus, or is it just the effort and imagining of a well intentioned soul trying to evangelize in the Lord's behalf. Or, worst case scenario, is it a real message from the wrong spirit?

Someone once told me, "Satan could even screw up a one car funeral." Kinda lousy language, but the point is well taken. Believe it.

Condemnation, Sanction, Or Caution?

Part of the good news of the past 18 months concerning the Marian Movement and the apparition business is that the Church finally got around to taking a position on some of these private revelations. On the one hand, we have to applaud the Church's patience and caution in her discernment of private revelation as discussed in the first sections of this book. On the other hand, we have to wonder at her silence in the face of such overwhelming evidence either in favor of, or in opposition to some of these claimed apparitions, messages and devotions.

The next issue is, when she has made a statement or ruling, what did it really say; what does it really mean?

The first issue is "sanctions." Sanction is one of those crazy, English-language words that can have completely opposite meanings. It sends one running for the dictionary. In these issues, we can usually assume that "sanctions" is not an endorsement of some visionary or apparition site. It is opposed to.

A "condemnation" means shut it down. And a "caution" is usually the avenue taken in the early going. Medjugorje falls under the caution criteria. To add to the time delay in getting these things either approved or shot down, we seem to get the terms "negative judgment" and "caution" interwoven.

The guidelines prepared by Cardinal Seper of the Holy See, as described earlier in this book, spell out some of the steps that need to be taken by the local Chancery involved, the category of findings, and how they are stated. An apparition may be judged either:

- There is nothing supernatural here, but we aren't condemning the messages or the people or devotions involved.
- We have not yet established anything supernatural here, and as such are suspending devotions, pilgrimages, etc.
- We have not yet established the supernatural here, but are authorizing the continued devotions, liturgies, pilgrimages, etc. (Medjugorje).
- We do not want the faithful, or the Church to have anything to do with these claimed messages, devotions, or the visionary involved (Necedah, Bayside, Vassula).

Medjugorje could possibly have fallen into this last category if Bishop Zanic had his way early on. Immense stumbling blocks evidently existed as to such a ruling based on the fact that he first approved, then disapproved, and finally tried to condemn the entire thing before his own investigative committee could even take a position. Also, the consistency of the messages remains, over periods of many years, in spite of great difficulties.

The seers are still there, and without seeking worldwide fame and fortune. And finally, the spiritual conversions are greater there than anything the Church has seen in the past thirty to forty years.

It is probably also fair to note here that there is little question but that certain elements in the Church (many bishops internationally and those in high places in the Holy See) would love to see Medjugorje condemned. There is probably a belief that such a move would put an end to all of these crazy apparitions and fanatic Marian supporters around the world. Perhaps there is a need to read what Gamaliel had to say about trying to do in the work of the Lord (*Acts* 5:33-40). He warned the Sanhedrin:

> *"So now I tell you, have nothing to do with these men and let them go. For if this activity is of human*

*origin, it will destroy itself. But if it comes from God,
you will not be able to destroy them; you may even
find yourself fighting against God.*

Joseph Januszkiewicz in Marlboro, New Jersey; Vassula
Ryden; Maria Paula of California; the events at Medway,
Massachusetts; Dr. Mary Jane Even, from Nebraska; Tony
Fernwalt from Akron, Ohio; and Theresa Lopez from Denver have all received some form of the above actions by the
Church against their claimed supernatural manifestations.
Another would be Cyndi Cain, formerly from Arkansas;
however, it is doubtful the Chancery in Little Rock will
make the information public knowledge. Lubbock, Texas,
would be an example of a very quick sanction against the
reported apparitions, but where much of the same manifestations are still taking place. Other sites claim the same.

Maria Paula's (Our Lady of the Rock) difficulties stemmed
from: widespread fund raising for a church, orphanage and
convent for a new order. The investigative commission, it
was reported, revealed she was not obedient to the request
not to have Mass said there, and she advised her board of
directors not to speak to the commission unless she first
approved what they were going to say. Prophecies included:
Rome would soon be destroyed by French, Italian, Russian,
Chinese and Japanese interests. Russia was now ready to
destroy the world, and the "Italian is prepared" (the belief
that the antichrist is an Italian already living in Rome and
ready to strike).

Anthony Fernwalt is a claimed visionary in the Kil-
gore/Akron area of Ohio. His messages are still being dis-
seminated, and reports of healings, (a new healing spring)
and other phenomena, continue to be reported there. In the
October 31, 1993 issues of *Mary's People*, it was reported that
the Bishop of Steubenville had stated: "We do not accept as
authentic his alleged apparitions and messages." The
Catholic Telegraph, newspaper of the Diocese of Cincinnati
also carried a major article on these events, including the
fact that there was some mental illness involved. There are
letters from the pastor of St. Jude's Orthodox Church, originally involved with Tony's apparitions, who have refuted
the entire thing, as well as from a mental health professional, and the statement (not verified) that the priest asso-

ciated with Tony as his spiritual director had been stripped of his faculties several years ago. A number of rather apocalyptic prophecies that were supposed to occur in 1992, did not happen.

The events at Medway, MA. were sanctioned by Cardinal Law in a statement of October 13, 1995. There was no case against Sr. Margaret Sims, founder of the apostolate, and who was involved with Maria Esperanza from Betania in bringing the Medway site into being. Though it apparently has not taken on the image of a "refuge," the site and the planned community to be built there involved millions of dollars, and was evidently showing signs of getting out of control. We applaud the Cardinal, and the people involved with this apostolate as well, for calling a "time-out" to the proceedings.

On September 26, 1993, *Our Sunday Visitor* published an article stating that Bishop John Reiss of Trenton, New Jersey, had released a ruling against the claimed apparitions of Joseph Januszkiewicz in Marlboro. It caused some negative response to the bishop and Joseph stated Our Lady did not want to "move" the apparition site from his home and the residential neighborhood as requested by the bishop. The bishop's position was stated in a 1,200 word statement.

In May of 1995, the Diocese of Lincoln, Nebraska, released a statement regarding the claimed seer, Dr. Mary Jane Even, who is known as "the Secretary of Jesus and Mary." This negative judgment referenced the "eccentric and farfetched nature of some of the materials in her writings." Those who have read any of the several dozen booklets of messages this seer published knows full well the meaning of the above statement from the bishop. Involved were alleged heavenly messages that included: Communion in the hand is condemned. Women must cover their heads in church. Follow any seer you believe in, regardless of what a bishop says. The Renew program is of the devil. All seers should be under one head and should be united to "The Little Pebble." Both Jesus and Mary will judge souls. Many who die are called back to earth to work. The rapture has already begun and many will be taken alive to Paradise. Jesus can never be present on an altar if the priest is a woman. List of true seers was made public in the Fall of 1993. Only certain states are safe havens. Refuge centers are "Heaven's Glen."

The messages also stated Jesus demanded tabernacles and statues put back, and He put down priests and bishops heavily. The above referenced mailing list of true seers was indeed a fact. It was sent out by the Little Pebble, a totally bizarre, claimed seer from Australia who states he is to be the next Pope. It came as no surprise that the "true seers" listed were those principally aligned to him.

Not to be outdone, another apparition (California) included a message that the Holy Spirit was really St. Joseph. Vassula Ryden's difficulties have received a lot of press lately and probably do not need to be covered here in detail. In summary, there were questions as to her messages involving the Blessed Trinity, that misinterpreted word "unity," the role of the World Council of Churches in our future, receiving the Sacraments as a non-Catholic, the whole "automatic writing" thing, plus a few other items. Personally, I always felt there was something very frightening about any visionary who had the capability to mesmerize a following (particularly priests and bishops), or who tried so hard to look like Jesus.

The material concerning Cyndi Cain (Bella Vista, Arkansas) will probably not be released by the Chancery in Little Rock. They were content to just have Cyndi and Michael move out of state. At issue there are many prophecies that were incorrect, endless passages from the wrath of God and promised chastisement, the fact that He will deal harshly with anyone who doubts His messengers, messages at odds with Church practice, questions of money and profit, and the big issue of the "refuge center" and a new religious order.

Additional information regarding the events surrounding Cyndi and Vassula are included in other segments of this book and in the appendix.

On March 8, 1992, Archbishop J. Francis Stafford, of Denver, Colorado, issued a statement which basically stated the alleged apparitions of Theresa Lopez were devoid of any supernatural origin. He also directed the faithful to refrain from participating in or promoting para-liturgical or liturgical services related to the alleged apparitions, among other sanctions.

There is always a definite need to applaud not only such action of the Church, but the total charitable nature in which these sanctions are presented. Such was the case with the statements of Bishop Stafford, and by his Vicar General and Moderator, Rev. Raymond Jones. On the other hand, there is a very definite need for the laity to know what had transpired, and why. It is not a case of trying to expose a visionary, or defame someone. It is a case of putting definitive facts into the hands of hundreds of thousands of people who are being overrun with claimed private revelations and don't know what to do about it. In the face of the overtime efforts of Satan to destroy the Marian Movement, this information is now vital today. The same must be said regarding Vassula; Cyndi Cain; Mary Jane Even; Bayside, New York; Marlboro, New Jersey; or Akron, Ohio. Why was it approved, or why wasn't it; that's the issue.

The rest of the information regarding Theresa Lopez included past marriages, the fact that some of the material she claimed as coming from Jesus or Mary came from other books (including one of ours for the "Chaplet of Virtues"), some questions concerning the involvement of Bishop Hnilica, and the content of the consecration book, *In the End My Immaculate Heart Will Triumph*. This book had some departures from what most of us learned concerning the Catholic faith. Briefly, in the book Our Lady states:

> *I ask you now to place your concentration on my heart only ... I am always present before you.*
> *I have said, I shall give all to you. This is my solemn promise. You need only what is found within me.*
> *I give the intensity of this grace ... to find in me, only in me, your solidarity and your sense of direction.*
> *Look to find only what I have taught you ...*

One of the problems here was evidently the fact that Mary is everything and provides all—as indicated above. The book echoes Bishop Hnilica's statements that Mary will provide all, including the statement: "Thus, in this way and **only** in this way shall they be drawn . . ." The potential difficulty with all of that is better shown on page 43 of the book in the statement:

> "According to His majesty, He gave to her by grace, all the same rights and privileges which He possesses by nature. It is from this union of their hearts, that she would never be given less. It is in this heavenly union that Jesus, by His place within the Trinity, gives to Our Lady the divine graces to share of Himself completely and in **equal** measure" (my emphasis).

In this apparent devotion to Our Lady, seemingly giving her all of the power of the Trinity, the Diocese of Denver evidently also had negative feelings toward the fact that the book was not submitted to Cardinal Mahoney, the local Ordinary where the publisher is located, for an "Imprimatur." The publisher then acquired an official statement from Msgr. John Rhode as the Episcopal Vicar of the Santa Barbara Pastoral Region. The letter included the statement that the referenced book complied with the teachings of the Roman Catholic Church. Monsignor Rhode is since deceased, I believe, so there is no chance to pursue that. He was also involved with the claimed apparitions taking place in Santa Maria, California, and acted as the spiritual advisor to the seers there. This primarily involved Barbara Mathias, a visionary. In any case, in a letter received by this author, dated April 6, 1994, from Rev. Edward Buelt, a Vice Chancellor in the Denver Diocese, Father Buelt seems to not share Monsignor Rhode's convictions as to the consecration book.

Somewhere, it was reported that Theresa Lopez is now living in Rome under the protection of the Pope. I think you can pretty well scratch that. She did move to Rome and was living under the guidance of Bishop Hnilica, and I assume that is still the case. Regardless, that is of little value here, and I wish Theresa well for her future, and that of her family. As with so many other claimed mystics, we have a continual need to pray for them, and for God's direction and mercy, not for any condemnations.

Refuge Centers

One of the more troubling new aspects in this crescendo of private revelation is the promotion of refuge centers. The claimed need for these centers (according to Mary, or Her Son) is the imminent chastisement the world is to suffer (which it probably will). All of this is greatly enhanced by the publishers of material that cater to sensationalism, and who refuse to "let God be God" in the course of mankind's history.

The concept of "refuge centers," "safe havens," "Heaven's Glen," "centers for her chosen remnant," is to herd the faithful to specific areas of the country where they will be safe and will live in community like the early Church. One of the first difficulties encountered is that not all visionaries agree on this concept, or where the centers should be. Dr. Mary Jane Even laid it out in detail, listing a number of regions of several midwest states that were now designated as Heaven's Glens.

A spin off from this concept has been the sudden increase in the purchase of land and the development of sanctuaries, retreat houses, prayer centers, or just farms for future designation, as commanded by Our Lord or Our Lady to a chosen messenger.

I believe the first reaction to such projects has to be: "good idea! We could certainly use more of that."

The second reaction might be a little more realistic:

> Who is promoting this, and for what reason?
> Has the Church stamped a big "approval" sign on it?
> Does that mean that somewhere down the road parishes have been stripped of parishioners? Or that a cult has formed?

Then there is the simple fact that I do not believe the Blessed Virgin Mary is in the real estate development business any more than she is in the book publishing business, regardless of our efforts today to put her in both. We also seem to have come to the point where we believe she wishes to run businesses, appoint executives, name companies and ministries, and engage in international commerce. I doubt it.

David Koresh had a form of refuge center in Waco, Texas. Elizabeth Claire Prophet is the great guru of the sect out west that has thousands of people and complete underground facilities they claim will withstand the coming chastisement (unless the Lord decides otherwise—a possibility they often seem to miss). Emmett Culligan (the water softener company) wrote a book in the 1950s on the coming end times and moved his family to a retreat/bunker in Montana. I remember my father-in-law (Ray Riehle, founder of the Foundation) was infatuated with that concept as he was also concerned over the plight of the world.

Refuge centers seem to be a product of "the end times" thinking, and of "reading the signs of the times." It appears to be prominent in all Christian thinking and even Scriptural passages that allude to it. In Catholic circles it seems to be rooted more in private revelation. We can go all the way back to the messages of La Salette, and work our way forward, and lay out a pretty complete profile for the need for a refuge center for all of us. The second half of this century has seen an explosion of gloom and doom prophecy, starting with Garabandal, up through Akita, Japan, and into this decade where we have a claimed "messenger" in every state in the country providing us with messages of imminent chastisement.

Let's start by laying out one basic concept here. People are attracted to, or follow the development of refuge centers, based on the claimed (from a seer) approval by the Lord, or His Mother. Someone has claimed a message from the Heavenly requesting the people to do this. The negative side is that you (if you move there or support it) are always going to be under the domain of that seer who can always produce a message for some desired action or decision. If the entire thing is truly of God, no problem. If it isn't, there will always be a "message" to evoke the desired result.

Marv Kucera is a visionary in Iowa. He has had several books published on his messages (principally from Jesus). In reading Marv's material you would tend to believe he is a very spiritual, humble and religious man, and that Marv totally believes in what he is doing. He deserves our prayers.

He reports that He has been commissioned by the Lord to

set up twelve refuges in this country, being the twelve tribes of Israel. Some, he says, are established and some remain hidden. He took this concept to various Marian organizations across the country and has been trying to establish these twelve new tribes of Israel for the past five years. One of these refuge centers is known as "Faithful and True" in New Hampshire. Originally, the Faithful and True apostolates were linked with the Little Pebble and the claimed visionary, "Trumpeter of the Apocalypse," as well as with Bayside.

Two volumes of Marv's books of messages are extremely chastisement oriented and often get promoted for the sensationalism included in many of the messages. Jesus soundly chastises His priests while stating He is providing a "New Covenant" and the "Ark of the Greater Testament." He says there is no need to go through Church authority anymore. One can find great empathy for Marv in these books as he seems to be constantly shot down by the Lord over one thing or another. Regardless, given the material contained in the book, one might want to question, or least seriously investigate the concept of these refuge centers.

Peter Christopher Gruters is a claimed visionary from Florida. A couple of years ago he, along with his brothers, were involved in the Divine Will efforts in Florida when he started receiving messages, again, principally from Jesus. Our Lord became the principal promoter and publishing agent for the books and several editions have been produced. Peter became supported by a gentleman from Dayton (by virtue of a message for him), and several other persons, including a priest, at a special "unity" meeting in Virginia at the site of another refuge operated by John Downs. There are approximately nine families now involved in the new refuge/community project in St. Mary's Ohio, where the group moved to.

Reports from the Diocese in Florida, as to the background of this seer and group involved, provided some angry and not very positive results. Much of the material in the books, and the development of this apostolate again seems to come from the seer having a message for whoever it was that needed to become involved. He also had some strong messages and prophecies for certain other visionaries and apparition sites that are highly questionable.

The demise of a refuge/lay community in Virginia was

also attributed to the "unity" issue, and some very bad prophecy. John Downs is a very religious and admirable man who has performed yeoman work for the Lord in spite of severe physical handicaps. He started this community in Virginia and became involved in extensive promotion of the Rosary among other things. We had worked with John with materials for a couple of years on a Rosary Congress in the Washington D.C. area. Several years ago this community became a site for its own apparitions/locutions and John believed he was called to unite all Marian apostolates under his control from the Virginia location. Certain attempts to advise him otherwise were not successful and instead, certain prophecies by questionable visionaries were followed to proceed with the planned new organization.

Suffice it to say, the results were not positive. It was possibly during this meeting of various Marian Apostolates, that Peter Gruters linked up with a former staff member of Catholic Relief Services, the aforementioned gentleman from Dayton, who was then involved with a claimed visionary from the Cleveland area (who had also received a message for him to become involved in her ministry), and a priest who would serve as spiritual advisor. Thus a new apostolate was in place for the distribution of the Gruter books and the eventual move to Ohio to establish a new refuge there.

A somewhat tragic example of a refuge center/new community project was the one in Arkansas. The visionary involved was Cyndi Cain, known also as the Hidden Flower. Largely through the journalistic talents of her husband, Michael, the Cains produced a very successful newsletter/newspaper titled "A Call to Peace." It features excellent articles, many from a number of prominent priests or nuns who appear to be affiliated with this ministry and the newsletter. They aren't. The past five years have produced an extensive list of messages Cyndi claims to have received from Our Lady, or Jesus, which are printed in the newspaper/newsletter. Many included prophecies and specific events which have proved to be wrong, and the material is extremely apocalyptic. In that vein a refuge center was announced, and the entire procedure was covered by specific messages from Our Lady, guaranteeing its success. In

1993, a number of families were relocating to Sulphur Springs, Arkansas.

In 1994, a number of Marian apostolates and publishers started receiving letters and materials indicating that all was not well in Arkansas. Those then living on the site were doubting the authenticity of the seer's locutions and stating that every decision which took place there had a specific message from Our Lady as a directive. A spiritual advisor to the seer, and to the refuge center group, dropped out of the entire affair—quietly. Hundreds of thousands of dollars were involved, careers up-ended, homes sold, families moved from other states. Legal action was initiated. Reports supplied from the Arkansas location indicated much of the material included in the messages as to the establishment of the center, a new order of nuns, personal meetings with the Pope who would also personally endorse the new order, a supposed brother and a supposed nun who were to be in charge, etc., etc. either were not correct or did not happen. Other messages indicated "Eucharistic Communities" (which this was supposed to be) would be centers of "His true presence." This new order was announced in 1991 and was to be immediately blessed by John Paul II since the "seventh seal" would be opened in 1992, which was to be the last days of the end times.

The Chancery in Little Rock, Arkansas, confirmed that an investigation was in process, that all of the reported charges seemed to be true, and indeed many thousands of dollars were involved (not to mention lost careers and homes). It was hoped the Chancery would issue a public statement as to their findings, not to expose a visionary or a bad situation, not to point fingers of condemnation at Cyndi, but for the sake of hundreds of thousands of people who subscribe to that paper, or who follow those messages, or who support that refuge center or others which were now starting up at other locations, and as a guideline for discernment in this exploding issue of private revelation. People needed Church direction—and there wasn't any.

Subtly, and indirectly, the Chancery took the position that they were sure the seer would now move out of state, and the whole thing would just go away, and thus an unpleasant episode could be avoided.

Future issues of "A Call to Peace" newsletter, from the point where it all started to come apart, said that great attacks were underway by Satan to undermine the entire apostolate, that the ground had become contaminated by his efforts, that the seer was now a suffering servant, that the bishop was unfairly doubtful, and that the Lord wanted them to move from that place. I believe there was a settlement of 10¢ on the dollar toward the failed refuge. The seer's messages suddenly stopped and the Cains moved to the Dallas, Texas area.

Do you feel a need to support the planned construction of a new retreat center? Or a shrine? Or a refuge center or some planned new lay/religious community? Praise God! That's great. We all have a need to support these ministries and to add to the glory of God and His kingdom here on earth by continuing to build visible testimonials to His presence, and that of the Blessed Virgin Mary. And there are certainly so many, many worthwhile efforts out there right now to support.

But before you do, question it! Discern! Find out where the Church is with the whole thing. Let God be God. A visionary never will be.

Unity

One of the more interesting words being widely circulated in the area of private revelation today is the word "unity." It is something we all want, something the world needs, something many seers claim messages for, and something specifically called for by Jesus, Himself: "*That all may be one ... as you Father are in me and I in you*" (*John* 17:21-22). It is also a word that is a little confusing and somewhat controversial.

To Vassula, Mirna in Damascus, Theresa Lopez, and a half-dozen other prominent alleged visionaries, unity is a prime part of the message. To Medjugorje seers, it is as well, but only to a point. To Josyp Terelya and Father Gobbi, it is a no-no. To Bishop Hnilica it is vital, but only to the conversion of Russia, and for the unity of all Marian apostolates and ministries to be under his control.

Following are a number of direct quotations taken from a well-done, professional, four-page brochure on the great need for unity in the world. In part, it states:

"We, humanity as a whole, are learning the hard way that we all go up together, or we all go down together. International unity is fast becoming a necessity even for the strongest nations ... We can have international unity and, as a result, world peace, if we recognize:
That we are all one family under God ...
Our interdependence and need for cooperation in a modern world ...

"It is no longer possible to separate human affairs from spiritual reality and selfless living. The changing of the old order, the awakening of humanity to new possibilities and the purification of the political and economic arena, are today the factors of the greatest spiritual value ...

"An intelligent and cooperative public opinion must be developed in every land and this constitutes a major spiritual duty ...

"The human and world crisis of today is basically spiritual, testing the character and intention of all men and women. This provides opportunity to reappraise the values we accept as a personal standard of behaviour." And so on.

All pretty neat sounding stuff, and it continues on pleading with humanity for unity as a spiritual necessity today. Where do you think that brochure came from? Sound a lot like some of the Bill Clinton homilies? Well, actually that's very close. It is put out by **Lucis Trust**, one of the most openly occult organizations in the world. Lucis Trust is a product of Madame Blavatsky and Alice Bailey, occultists and New Age gurus who have written many books on those two topics, including the material accepted as the New Age handbook. The Satanic interests of Lucis Trust are well known and their supporters include some of the most prominent individuals and foundations in the world. Also included within their scope of influence is the United Nations.

The above referenced brochure goes on to point out that the answer to all of the above needs is already there for us, and it isn't Jesus Christ. The brochure goes on to state:

"The United Nations, through the General Assembly, specialized agencies, and its various councils, commissions and committees, must be supported; there is, as yet, no other organization to which we can hopefully look."

There is one other prominent entity that desires complete world unity and his initials are SATAN. Interestingly, it is also the goal of Lucis Trust and the United Nations: One world order, one world monetary system, and one world religion—his religion. There is a very urgent need to question, and to discern: just what are you uniting for, and with whom, and to do what? The other question is: what do you have to give up to achieve it?

Interestingly, as I am writing this (the end of May, 1996), I just noticed an article in the current issue of *The Wanderer*. Konrad Raiser, general secretary of the "Ecumenical Council of Churches," during an interview in Frankfurt, Germany, stated: "The Papacy is the biggest obstacle to greater Church unity." He went on to criticize the Catholic Church's policy "of allowing ecumenical contacts on its own terms, and therefore there can be no unity between the Ecumenical Council of Churches and the Catholic Church." Which brings us to the apparitions of Mirna, from Damascus.

Mirna Nazour is a claimed visionary with very heavy credentials, including the stigmata, and icons that ooze a sweet oil continuously. Her messages speak of "unity." So strong was some of her following in this regard that it even prompted Fr. Robert Fox to state: "Miracles like this for unity have not been seen since Our Lord Jesus and His Apostles walked in the Holy Land." Well, maybe not quite.

In any case, controversy surrounded Mirna, unfortunate indeed, if in fact she is an authentic visionary. Most of the controversy involved the author of her book, *The Miracle of Damascus*. The author is known as "The Publican." Mirna's promoters are a group known as the "Messengers of Unity." In the process, "unity" somehow got confused with money and power, maybe even a need to neutralize the Pope.

The book was promoted at $17.95, plus extensive postage charges, included several different *"Imprimaturs"* from alleged Catholic and Orthodox sources, and finished with the premise that to reach unity, it may be necessary for the Pope to step down. The author of the book, The Publican, had also written a book titled *The Tongues of Satan*, which was an open condemnation of any charismatic. He also states he can identify all false mystics and apparitions, is a Biblical scholar, and completely knows the master plan of Satan. He knows which weeping statues are false, and also has the complete blueprint for the end times and the great chastisement (which includes seven years to just bury the dead). All of that can become a reason for casting some serious doubts on the whole affair.

Eventually some linked Mirna's messages with Vassula, another promoter of the unity theme, along with Theresa Lopez and Daniel Lynch with the "King of All Nations" promotions. A few others were brought on board, including "Debra" from Australia.

It was pretty much downhill from there on in, including Church sanctions against Vassula and Theresa Lopez. Rick Salbato (the author known as The Publican) placed statements in newspapers (*The Wanderer*, Oct. 26-95) disclaiming his own book, *The Miracle of Damascus*, due to the uncertain elements connected with the Imprimaturs and supposed church approvals that are contained therein.

Within a matter of weeks after the Vatican issued its statement concerning the alleged visionary, Vassula, new movements were underway to attempt to overturn it all. I have received phone calls, letters, and faxes circulating petitions in defense of Vassula, and a copy of a letter addressed to Joseph Cardinal Ratzinger that basically says: We are right. You are wrong. And we will defend Vassula to the end. You cannot tell us what to do.

The company that produces Vassula's materials issued a publication including new messages of Vassula, from Jesus, defending Vassula (naturally), and also articles by several priests refuting the Holy See. Is what you see here the early beginnings of a cult?

And this is the fruit of unity?

Anyone who has been following private revelation for the past ten years or so may recognize a very important and common trait here. In every case, where there is question about the authenticity of a visionary, or the acceptability of his or her messages, we can find additional messages or statements from the visionary stating that Satan is trying to destroy the whole thing, or that she will be attacked and ridiculed. It was there constantly with Nancy Fowler, with Cyndi Cain, with Theresa Lopez, Denise Morgan Estrada, etc. And it is now coming from Vassula's camp. The cry will always be that Satan's efforts are to try and destroy the unity that the messages are producing. Maybe so. On the other hand, maybe what we see now is the real fruit of the wrong messages.

We all must decide.

The other area of "unity" being tossed around today—and has been for the past eight or nine years—is the effort to unite all visionaries, and all Marian organizations. It has been attempted several times, with limited results. The unification of visionaries was meagerly attempted a few years ago with a group in the western part of the United States (Harriet Hammons, Veronica Garcia, Theresa, Denise, Carol Ameche, among others). Internationally, the Little Pebble (Australia) did indeed attempt such a coup, with himself at the helm, naturally, and produced and mailed out a very impressive list of claimed seers from all over the world, in 1992 and 1993. He even qualified the list by stating which were "true," which were "false."

The concept of unification of the entire Marian Movement, the consolidation of all Marian apostolates and centers, and providing a central headquarters for this massive entity has always been an interesting concept to me, and one which I could never make up my mind on. I pray about it (maybe not enough). But I still am not sure if it is a good idea or not.

Perhaps much of the doubt comes from the fact that Our Lady does not seem to endorse the idea. It seems to always be "our" idea, not hers. During this past ten years she has seemed to have called thousands. New ministries and apostolates have sprung up all over the world. Prayer groups grew by leaps and bounds. She has seemed content to do it all, area by area, parish by parish, ministry by ministry. Has she ever asked to unite them all? Or is she content to convert us all, one person at a time?

Regardless, in the past couple years a major attempt was initiated to do just that. *United for the triumph of the Immaculate Heart* is the apostolate instigated by Bishop Paolo Maria Hnilica to accomplish this. Those involved in the Marian Movement in this country have probably already been exposed to the bishop's credentials so there is no need to go through it all again here. I do not belong to or support this organization. Nor do I oppose it. I can only state why I am not involved.

The United for the Triumph apostolate, as a matter of stated policy, exists to provide direction and unity to the Marian Movement. Since it has become all too obvious that dissension, confusion, and some very questionable private revelation exists in the movement today, that can probably be perceived as a worthwhile goal. The problem might be that, like so much else in the field of private revelation, there is a whole bunch of hype, and very little discernment. Such might be the case here.

This new apostolate, headquartered in Rome, began its American operations under Denis Nolan. Denis is a friend, an example of commitment, and a gem in the Marian Movement. If Denis has a weakness (as we all do), it is probably his enthusiasm. He identified the bishop as "the right arm of the Holy Father," and Mary's appointed shepherd to lead the movement. I applaud Denis' commitment, but I'm not sure that statement is right. Seems like a lot of people want to be identified as the Pope's right hand man.

I also saw a statement in a publication that warned that Marian Apostolates not united through the Bishop's apostolate won't be able to survive the trial soon to come upon the Church. An additional claim (and concern) was the status the bishop gave to the proposed new dogma on Mary as "Coredemptrix, Mediatrix of All Graces, Advocate." On the surface, it was easy to jump on board this victory train, complete with a new engineer, all united for the Triumph of the Immaculate Heart to be proclaimed any day now. Behind the scenes, the call for unity was already producing some disunity. And we already have enough.

Some have inquired as to Bishop Hnilica's past. At issue was his involvement several years ago in a Vatican Bank scandal (supposedly he has since been cleared), support of Vassula, and Theresa Lopez, his use of her apostolate and the questionable consecration book associated with it for his goals and objectives concerning Russia, the apparent dissatisfaction of some American bishops involved, etc.

Personally, I have little concern with all of that. Nor can you just throw in guilt because of mere association. No, its the discernment thing again—some questions that can be asked—that should be asked, before we all hop on the train to the triumph. These are the statements from the United for the Triumph apostolate that some feel need to be addressed:

- It is only by turning our attention to Russia that America will save itself.
- Our Lady's triumph coming out of Russia is the **only hope** for peace in the world.
- The bishop made a pledge (in 1951) to pursue the proclaiming of "this final dogma" and took up the cause of a visionary in Holland named Ida, who promoted messages for this dogma.
- The Pope, **united with all the bishops of the entire Catholic Church**, made the consecration originally called for from Fatima on March 25, 1984. (Many do not believe all bishops took part).
- God presents Our Lady as the true and **only** solution to the problems of the entire world.
- She **alone** can obtain for us the greatest gift—peace.
- The only refuge given by God for these times . . . the true remedy. (Mary).
- To be part of the coming triumph, it is alleged that you need to be under "the guidance of the bishop." This is specifically stated to mean:
  —Commitment to the place of Russia in the salvation of the world.
  —Ready to accept any humiliation that will come your way after you decide to work for the triumph.
  —Total and deep trust in the bishop.
  —Only one plan: The Triumph, and to concentrate all your efforts toward it.
  —To focus on the conversion of Russia and eastern Europe.

—To spread the message of Mary as CoRedemptrix, Mediatrix and Advocate.

—To be in complete obedience to the bishop and the efforts of the apostolate.

Bishop Hnilica makes a passionate plea for unity. And rightly so. He tells us to come together. He states our hope is totally in the conversion of Russia and Eastern Europe. That we must unite with the Orthodox churches. He pledges he is devoted to these causes.

Perhaps it needs to be studied further in that our commitment and obedience rests with the Holy Father and the Magisterium of the Church, not with private revelation or the rebuilding of Russia. It has nothing to do with putting down the bishop's goals. It has everything to do with priorities.

Secondly, there may be a need to question some of the hype on this supposed "final" dogma, the claims being attached to it by the bishop's apostolate, and the powers they are giving to Our Lady. I love and honor this lady, maybe more than you do. But if Mary is the **only** hope for the world, the **only refuge;** if she **alone** can obtain for us the gift of peace; if the salvation of the world has been totally put in her hands, then the salvific mission of Jesus Christ wasn't necessary. Then His suffering and death on the cross was a waste of time. Then devotion to His most Sacred Heart, the Eucharist, the pleas He made to Sister Faustina to seek out His Divine Mercy, are all just secondary issues.

I don't think so.

Do we have all of this in the proper perspective here? Magazines, newspapers, newsletters, and books and videos have been pumping this up now for a couple of years. In the process, have we elevated this humble, handmaid of the Lord beyond where she really wants to be? Have we put private revelation and someone else's ministry above the teaching authority of the Church? Let God be God!

A New Dogma?

The reality of this concern can be seen in some of the promotion being given to a proposed new Marian dogma which would officially title Our Lady as "Coredemptrix, Mediatrix, Advocate." This effort was spearheaded by Mark I. Miravalle, S.T.D., Professor of Theology and Mariology at the Franciscan University of Steubenville, who authored a book by that title in May of 1993.

I am privileged to be personally acquainted with Mark Miravalle. Not only is he a highly respected leader in his field, he is a totally committed son of Our Lady and is dedicated to the Pope and the Magisterium of the Church. I personally have no specific problems with the proposed dogma. The titles, as listed above are already titles of Mary that have been used for many years. Earlier in this book, I made mention of a book titled *Mary, Mother of the Church*, by Fr. Francis Ripley, and published by TAN Books and Publishers, Inc., Rockford, Illinois. This book gives extensive attention to Mary under many titles, including the three listed above, and quotes from Popes and Doctors of the Church supporting various titles given to Our Lady. If this petition to the Church for a new dogma comes to pass, I for one will have no trouble in accepting it.

I think there is a whole lot to be concerned with in the manner it is being presented however. This is not fair to Mark Miravalle, or to the Church, and is certainly not the way Mark presented his case. His was a very scholarly treatment of the subject. What we are getting now, like so much of the material being put out in the name of claimed visionaries everywhere, is the embellishment of the proposed dogma, and to its detriment.

It has become very obvious in the past five years that claimed visionaries are prone to hop on specific new issues in the Marian Movement and quickly produce a "message" confirming such and such or so and so. No sooner did this booklet from Mark Miravalle come out (at the Notre Dame Medjugorje Conference that year), then messages of confirmation were provided. The question is: were they messages to support the book, or messages to pump up the image of a visionary? Were not some also used to show that the book supported some seer's claim that he/she had received such a request from the heavenlies previously?

The above material dealing with "unity" and Bishop Hnilica's apostolate can again be used to emphasize the point. Not only are other visionaries distributing messages in support of the proposed doctrine, but they have a tendency to add to it. In some cases, "Co-redemptrix" (small "r") became

"Co-Redeemer," "Advocate" becomes "Advocate of **all**
graces" hinting at the elimination of the need for Jesus and
the Holy Spirit in the process. Mary becomes the **only** hope,
the **only** refuge. New books and materials are introduced. A
seer in Phoenix states that Our Lady has requested that the
"Virgin of the Globe" medal now be struck to replace the
Miraculous Medal that was not made in accordance with
the original request. Promoters of the proposed dogma
became involved with the new medal which incorporates
the titles "Coredemptrix, Mediatrix, Advocate."

One visionary from the Philippines (where there are a
number of questionable seers), has now come out with a
new prayer for "Our Lady of the Eucharist," which indicates
that Mary is also present in the Host.

I think we need to once again recognize that: "this is private revelation, not Church teaching." I think our original
Miraculous medal is just fine; we don't need to fork out
some heavy bucks for some claimed new, high-powered
replacement. We also might want to confirm that there is
only one body on that crucifix, not two, and that Jesus said:
"This is my body," not this is our body. He alone came as the
Messiah. Should the Church elect to provide Mary with
additional titles and powers, praise God. But let's not run
away with the whole concept based on current private revelation from a number of seers, or on the claimed messages
of a lady named Ida who claimed visions in Holland forty to
fifty years ago, the main thrust of which were these "final"
titles to be given to Mary. Her visions have never been
approved by the Church.

Bishop Hnilica's endorsement of Ida, it appears, not only
gave impetus to the current seers on this subject, but it also
has given them the apparent knowledge that this is the
"final dogma." Who says? Why not two more? Why not two
hundred more? Should messages, newsletters, magazines,
and petitions now flying around, create additional powers,
a new medal, a "final dogma" and a whole new range of sensationalism attributed to this quiet lady of the Bible who
simply told us to *do whatever he tells you*?

I wonder if this is what Mark Miravalle had in mind? I
doubt it.

Simplicity Or Confusion

Isn't it truly amazing how we are apparently drifting away from what the Mother of Jesus has asked us to do? What a contrast! She keeps telling us to simplify our lives.

Medjugorje certainly has its critics. And their opposition is well noted, their points of contention accepted. Still, the messages of Medjugorje provide a certain stability and spiritual direction that almost all other current apparition sites lack. It is truly "spiritual soul food," not "spiritual entertainment." If you doubt it, go and see.

In Medjugorje the Virgin has consistently told us to: Pray, convert, fast, make Jesus the first priority in your lives, and **simplify your lives.** She keeps telling us to live her messages and simplify our lives, and somehow we seem to be interpreting that as meaning more books, more videos, more medals, more devotions, more apparitions and messengers, more apocalyptic warnings, more tours, and in the process we find only more and more confusion.

Satan also believes in God. In fact, he is a rebel from God's angelic legions. He is His enemy. He also is an expert on Scripture. He knows Catholic doctrines and devotions and what is being said at all authentic supernatural manifestations. He is infinitely cunning and deceptive, and certainly smart enough to know his presentation has to sound good and plausible or nobody is going to buy it. In doing so, he knows false apparitions and seers cause disunity and division and confusion between those who believe and those who don't. He knows he can draw people away from sound doctrine and truth by mixing in a few fables here and there to attract "itching ears." He knows the value (to him) in seeking after the sensational; and that multiplying prayers and new devotions can cause pressures and scrupulosity and guilt feelings, with eventual abandonment of the whole thing somewhere down the road, including good, solid, religious practices. Meaner than a junkyard dog.

In discussing discernment, I once had a priest tell me: "Bill, discerning apparitions is really not difficult. This is not brain surgery you know!" Well, that is absolutely right. It isn't brain surgery. It's much more difficult. Brain surgery deals with only the human element, with human skills, with the human body. Discerning apparitions and visions deals with the supernatural elements. Satan is a spirit, a being of the spirit world. As such, his powers are infinitely greater than yours if you take him on one-on-one. Without the grace of God, you are no match. He has the power to possess, to injure, to kill. Deception is his hallmark. Confusion is his strength.

Take time out to honestly evaluate what is going on in the Marian Movement today. There is much good. There are obviously authentic apparitions and seers. There is great strength. That is precisely why he is in the middle of it.

And that is the other message from the Virgin at Medjugorje. She has constantly warned of Satan's presence. Her answer, as always, is prayer, fasting, conversion. And she adds a request to dump all the sensationalism and economic greed, and instead, **simplify** your life. It comes with the admonition to: *Live my messages.*

Specific Messages And Messengers

Today you often hear that all of this must be true because all of these seers and messages are saying the same thing. That, folks, is pure poppycock. It simply is not true.

Let's use two very well known visionaries, Maria Esperanza and Estela Ruiz. The message from Betania was that the start of 1995 was to be a "time of the glory of God":

> "The beginning of 1995 we are going to see the glory of God like man has never experienced in the past . . . . The event will take place some time between the 15th and 20th of February. . . . The Lord would be coming and there will be a change of consciences . . . . There will be an explosion of graces felt all over the world and not just in Betania. . . ."

The messages from Estela did not indicate the beginning of 1995 to be a time of grace. Our Lady's message to her stated:

> "I came awhile back with messages of warning of imminent destruction of the world and to call you to conversion that this destruction might be avoided. . . . My words to you can no longer be of warning for now the world is in the middle of this

destruction. . . . Evil is loose all over the world and Satan devours my children. . . . These are evil times of battle and only our constant watch over your soul will keep this evil away. . . ."

If you wish to read 30 or so different message books from various seers, along with those of earlier generations and even earlier centuries, you will find that many of the current "sensationalism" books have simply picked up messages from parts of different books and put them together along with various passages from Scripture to compose a blueprint for the end-times, the purification, etc. Since a dozen different American visionaries put out several years worth of messages, we have no trouble finding a match in there somewhere to fit with the others. However, we will also find just as many contradictions. We can find countless predictions that were wrong, questionable theology, some absurd terminology and sensationalism, messages confirming other seers or other messages (which are questionable to begin with), the need for discernment (for other apparition sites, not their own), that there are many false seers today (but never any doubt about the one speaking), and as always the request to have the messages published. The end result can be mass confusion.

If you have any doubt about that statement, I have a job for you in our offices (a non-paying one, naturally). You can handle all the phone calls, the letters, and the faxes that come in continually, from all over, from people upset about some new message from some visionary somewhere, or questioning some new devotion, or some new predicted date for such-and-such to happen, etc., etc. It is not unusual to hear, or read, "I am so upset and confused about this. I want to do what Our Lady is asking of us, but I just feel so uncomfortable with this." More than one person has asked whether they should sell all and move to _____.

Following in this chapter is a list of message segments from various seers. All of this has been in print and is public knowledge. You read it, and you discern it. Most of this material comes from Nancy Fowler, Theresa Lopez, Denise Estrada, Louise Lahola, Marv Kucera, Maureen Sweeney, The Batavia Visionary and Rita Ring (from the Holy Spirit Center/Lady of Light Publications), Sadie Jarmillo, Cyndi

Cain, Dr. Mary Jane Even, and Carol Ameche. However, in total, dozens of visionaries, and different books are involved.

In a number of cases, Jesus or Mary request the visionary involved to read specific books, including the Douay-Rheims version of the Bible. Books include: "The Poem of the Man-God," (5 volumes), "God Calling," "God at Eventide," "He And I," "The Mystical City of God," "Mary, Day By Day," "Padre Pio, The True Story," "My Daily Bread," "On Fire With the Spirit," "Lord and Giver of Life," among others.

In a number of cases, Jesus or Mary tell the visionary involved that we are not to judge and should never try to disprove messages. Threats are even made through messages toward any that doubt. Basically, the visionary (and the reader) are being told not to discern. At the same time, either Jesus or Mary warn the visionary that there are many false prophets today, many false visionaries. How do you determine who they are if you are not to discern? The answer, obviously, is that whoever Jesus or Mary are supposedly speaking to at the time is a true messenger. This is especially true with several widely known, claimed seers. Of course, you are always free to promote their messages and divulge their names in the process, but you are never supposed to divulge their names in the case of some bad material, for this is considered "judging."

Message Excerpts

—*Those who choose not to come to Me now, My Little One, their pain will be multiplied a thousand times over.*

—*I come with a New Covenant. Cease your doubting. Build My refuges. There are many in your country I have spoken to about My refuges. Do you think they all can be wrong?*

—*When the winter months are past, great will be the chastisement upon your country* (Oct. 93)

—*If you decide on your own and condemn one of My prophets, and they are of Me, each of you shall pay a great price.*

—*My words will soon be made known in the books I have asked you to distribute.*

—*I have asked Twelve Places of Refuge be prepared, named after the Twelve Tribes.*

—*At My refuges, there is dissension and bickering between My faithful. My patience grows thin.*

—*The devil cannot read your thoughts.* (But to another visionary Our Lord apparently said: *Beware, the devil may get into your thoughts.*)

—*Here will I grant many healings. The blind will see, the deaf will hear, the lame will walk. Cancer and other ailments will be cured.*

—*You are to wear a new special medal which will allow you to identify Our Lord when he comes . . . Satan will also make a duplicate one.*

—*You are to write in the name of "Jesus Christ" on the election ballot.*

—*Children, if you do not believe this* (the messages), *then you stand accused before me.*

—(Jesus) *Some people are hearing messages in their heads but it is illusion.*

—*Questions are being asked of one another. Answers are being given to one another. Man thinks he has everything figured out. He thinks he can foresee the future and its happenings. Woe to the man who jumps ahead of me* (Jesus).

—*False prophets destroy what I have built by their promises.*

—(Jesus, regarding prophecies from others): *You do not need to read them.* (Our Lady): *There are many false messages. They are not coming from God. I am the Blessed Virgin Mary.*

—*All religious and priests and ministers are the same.*

—*These messages are to be added to revelation.*

—*Those who reject you* (the visionary), *reject me. All will be held accountable.*

—From Mary: *I will stop appearing to all my children during this coming year of grace* (1993).

—From Jesus: *Some I may ask, as My Mother has, to be obedient to priests and bishops—others, I will ask only for obedience to Me.*

—*It is important, I say to you, that girls not serve Me at the altar.*

—*Yes, my Little One, the time is now for the purification* (Aug. 6, 1994).

—After berating the visionary, Marv Kucera, for not getting the refuges built, Jesus states: *My refuges will be built in My time—not man's.*

—*Soon, a rumble will be heard across the land which will tear it in two* (June 94).

—(From the book *"As We Wait in Joyful Hope"*): *The beginning of tribulations in your country is about to unfold ... Death and violence will exist everywhere ... Even though there are new delays in some of His plans ... It is only a matter of minutes now on the Eternal Clock before more chaos erupts in the streets of your country ... The delays are meant to strengthen you and test your resolve ... New plans for the world are escalating the Father's justice ... The longer a period of waiting for these events the shorter will be the time spent experiencing them. You can save yourself so much grief and anxiety by refusing to speculate on events and the times of their fulfillment ... The hour of total abandonment is here ... Little time remains before ... an abyss of suffering and slavery ... The hour is nearly gone ... It will be a time of great cohesion among the members of My Mother's army ...*

—(Mary) *I now come to you in the same way to prepare you for this season of tribulation ... Your country will be under siege by nature ... Waters will know no bounds ... The mountains will erupt and the earth will shake ...* (Jan. 95).

—(Mary) *I come today to reassure you what I predict in this the season of tribulation is contingent upon the number of hearts that open ...* (In response to the message: *"The seasons will reverse themselves. The days and nights will be as one")* (Jan. 95).

—*The Triumph of My Immaculate Heart will begin today at Maranatha Spring* (May 94).

—Our Lady says, *"Concentrate on the message, not the messenger."* (Maureen Sweeney)

—*My children, the 900# is my humble invitation to all my little children to participate in the construction of the prayer center.* (A response from Our Lady about why she would request a 900 phone number at an apparition site. Under age 18 requires parental permission).

—*I desire that My Mother not only be honored by all of you, but that she also be accepted as My Coredeemer.* (Jesus to the Batavia Visionary).

—(Jesus) *Share this with my children. Have it printed and*

distributed. Do this immediately ... No more can My Father be merciful.

—(Jesus) *Sell your stocks, put away your investments . . . Money is worthless.*

—(Jesus) *Are you prepared for calamity ... The day is near for disaster to begin. Every hour should be spent in prayer ... I desire you to spend all of your waking hours in prayer.* (Aug. 92).

—(Mary) *Once you have given your heart to my Son, or to Me (We are one, for my Son is in me and I in my Son) ...*

—(Jesus: all from the same message). *The mercy of My Father is endless. He continues to pour His mercy onto mankind because of His endless love for all His creation ... Mercy is everlasting when it comes from the Father ... Soon, My Father's mercy will end.*

—(Jesus: to numerous visionaries). *Be prepared for attacks ... Be prepared to suffer much for my sake ... They will not believe you ...*

—(Jesus to Theresa Lopez). *Those who serve me shall never fail; those who explain me shall have everlasting peace ... I will allow no harm to come to you ...*

—(Mary) *I desire the women to remember not to receive Jesus uncovered, for this shows a lack of reverence.*

—(Jesus–in Canada). *We bless the book. Book sales skyrocket ... Make haste to publish. Leave the bishop to Us. We have Our way. It is so. Believe. Work on the shrine must begin posthaste.*

—(Jesus–in Canada). *My darling, the "Star of Bethlehem"* (newsletter) *grows. People are eager to subscribe. Keep the price but equal to the cost ... Omen, the Heavens rebuke any and all that would dare to obstruct the Star of Bethlehem.* (message of July 10, 1994). *The earthquakes begin. Heed the news. Rocks fall on the many and they are killed. Buildings collapse, yet envy and sloth prevail, all the deadly sins continue. Work! Fast! ... It is the Lord who speaks. The medal is of great value ...* (Message of June, 1994). *I am Our Lady of Mercy. The Word of God has come down upon you as to few other persons.*

—(Jesus) *Spend each moment of your waking conscience in prayer.*

—(Jesus) *Publish the next two books as I have just inspired you. The third book will be entitled "The March of Love,*

> *Heaven is on the Move." The fourth book will be "Volume*
> *II, His Kingdom Come, His Will Be Done"... My Son of My*
> *will, the book store idea was Mine, not yours ... Tell N. I will*
> *guide, I will direct, I will be the manager, I will be the*
> *administrator, for as he knows, he is not capable of any-*
> *thing himself ... (to Peter Gruters).*
> — (Jesus) *This is My Center, not yours ... stop blocking My*
> *will. Oh yes, the bishop said no donations, but you can*
> *take loans; let Me be the one who pays them off for you. My*
> *credit is good ... (to Peter Gruters).*
> — (Mary) *Ecclesiastical collegiality leads to chaos among the*
> *faithful and the Church leadership ... God's justice cannot*
> *allow the destruction of iniquity before it has come to*
> *maturity.*

In one book, Our Lady supposedly condemns ecumenism. She states, *"the dangerous ideology of a modern ecumenical Christianity is spreading."* In the same book she also states: *"May the Christians and all people of goodwill lay aside their religious hostilities, their political rivalry ..."*

Several years ago, Fr. Michael Scanlon, the President of Steubenville University, had an article that appeared in *Medjugorje Magazine* (a recommended publication). He was comparing the current Marian Movement with the difficulties confronted by the Charismatic Renewal a couple of decades ago. He noted that it "seems today many Mary devotees are involved in fervent devotion at apparition sites but do not necessarily become involved in a complete conversion experience which results in acceptance of Jesus as one's personal Lord and Saviour."

But most important, Fr. Michael, in his comparisons, seemed to hit the nail right on the head when he stated:

"Both movements suffer from 'spiritual inflation.' Just as early Charismatic Renewal prophecies and words of knowledge were given too much credence and too literal an interpretation, so many Marian inspirations are too quickly elevated to the status of locutions and visions."

Amen!

"Marian inspirations!" That covers a whole lot of ground. Including "Jesus inspirations" as well. I believe it is very important to recognize that there are probably many self-acclaimed locutionists and prophets who are not evil intentioned, but are simply over-zealous souls, committed to the Lord and/or His Mother, whose imaginations have run away with them. But in the Bible Peter tells us:

> *First you must understand this: there is no prophecy contained in Scripture which is a personal interpretation. Prophecy has never been put forward by man's willing it. It is rather that men impelled by the Holy Spirit have spoken under God's influence ... In times past there were false prophets among God's people, and among you also there will be false teachers who will smuggle in pernicious heresies ... They will deceive you with fabricated tales, in a spirit of greed* (*2 Peter* 1:20-21, 2:1-3).

To be sure, we must sadly report that we have some of that very much alive in the Marian Movement today. But by and large, most of the private revelation coming to us through this vast network of Marian communications probably has our best interest at heart. Unfortunately, its validity leaves a lot to be desired. In a recent book by Josyp Terelya, the Blessed Virgin Mary chastises Josyp for listening to false prophets of gloom and doom and states "Satan has scattered a multitude of false prophets who are dragging people down into the abyss." She then goes on to give prophecies of great peril and the arrival of armageddon. She assails ecumenism and refers to the Russian President as "Satan Yeltsin." The ideologies supposedly given by Mary seem to be those of Josyp.

The Blessed Virgin Mary, in addition to giving a Cleveland area visionary a "900 phone number" also produced a message that says we are to "judge the message, not the messenger." Well, I don't think so. The Church's criteria for judging the authenticity of apparitions involves the messenger as much as the message. It seems like we are now getting conflicting "message or messenger" importance, depending on the acceptability involved, or the credibility of the seer.

The messages from Conyers, Georgia are awash in contradiction. For example, Jesus supposedly tells the visionary, *"All priests are to hear this. All who reject you reject me."* Does that mean that Jesus doesn't believe in the Church teaching that no one is obliged to believe in private revelation? The claimed visionary is constantly given warnings of impending doom and at one such session Our Lord claims that *nowhere is there any reparation in the world.* Given the fact that Medjugorje has produced over 5,000 new prayer groups, millions of daily rosaries, and thousands of new Marian peace groups, one might question whether the visionary got that message right. On another occasion, Our Lord tells the visionary that some people are hearing messages in their head but it is all an illusion. But He tells her, *"you have mystical knowledge of God."*

In regard to that message of "where is reparation?" Jesus then goes on to say that our prayers and sacrifices are postponing a great war. He also stated that *there is no other place in the world where graces are being bestowed like here* (Conyers). That seems like a little much. You mean that at this "un-approved," claimed, apparition site, there are greater graces than at Lourdes? Or at Fatima? Or at adoration of the Blessed Sacrament in your own parish? Or greater than in actually receiving the Eucharist?

Our Lord allegedly told Denise Morgan Estrada: *Tonight will be the last night you have* . . . that she will be infallible . . . that the new Pope will be good, not the antichrist that other visionaries predict . . . the major earthquake (the big one) would take place in 1992 . . . If people do not listen to this, they are all going to hell . . . Communion in the hand must stop . . . etc., etc.

A Sr. Marie-Danielle, from the Canadian Order of the Immaculate Heart, supposedly under the direction of a Fr. Yves-Marie Blais, states that she: Is crucified on the cross every Friday . . . the pope comes to see her almost every night . . . has the crown of thorns but it is invisible . . . Canada and the United States will be invaded by Russia . . . Wears Fr. Blais's crucifix which is the most indulgenced crucifix in the world . . . and we must never judge mystics. Sr. Marie-Danielle, it turns out, was affiliated with the claimed Australian seer, "The Little Pebble" and supported by one of his apostolates, *Faithful and True of the Midwest.*

Messages coming out of California to several claimed seers there have long since passed the point of simply evoking questions. What started as an apparent, simple, devout movement, sparked by claimed messages to build a huge cross in the Santa Maria area, became invaded by a second seer named Barbara (and a mountain of conflicting documentation against), and wound up with a couple of more visionaries who have been giving messages about the final earthquake for California for three and one-half years.

A Deacon in the Church, in Georgia, reported messages in 1992, which included appearances from Mary in the Church after Mass. The messages stated a special sign would be given to the world on October 12, 1992 . . . (There was an earthquake in Egypt that day). There will be seven years of tribulation from that date . . . That all appearances of Mary would end in the year of grace (1993) and the rapture would then take place—or a form thereof. To a seer in Houston, Texas, 1994 or early 1995 was to be the end for all apparitions. It wasn't.

Many claimed visionaries stated that all of Our Lady's messages have stopped, or are about to stop. Others refute this. There may also be a need to question if there is some connection between certain visionaries who seem questionable, and certain devotions and/or titles of Jesus or Mary that evoke concern. For example, a claimed "voice box" (why does that identification cause great stress in me?), Franz Joseph Keiler, is, or was affiliated with "The Little Pebble," the seer "Thornbush," and the denounced seer, Mary Jane Even. He receives messages that include: *"You must receive the Eucharist from a priest only, kneeling, and on the tongue ... Children, you are going to receive many messages from heaven that are quite controversial. Believe me, they are from heaven"* . . . He also sees Mary wearing the Crown of Thorns, and she comes as "Mediatrix of all Graces, Co-Redemptrix" (naturally).

A number of visionaries confirmed the February 17, 1994 date for the earthquake that would wipe out California. They also confirmed the date that "evil would be ripped out of the world" in 1995, the Pope's death, the chastisement, and the major warning to take place in Garabandal. God bless them for their faith, their commitment, their zeal to spread the "good news" to mankind, and their efforts for the conversions of sinners. Still, most of the time they are all wrong.

Even a claimed seer from the country of Pope John Paul II, Poland, was in the spotlight in a grand way. Wladyslaw Biernacki is known all over Europe. It is claimed that the Magisterium of the Church eagerly sought his advice when Cardinal Wyszynski, Primate of Warsaw, died in 1979 and a replacement needed to be named. Biernacki was also supposed to be very close to the Holy See, a personal friend and advisor to John Paul. Sometimes I feel there are only a few left who are not personal friends or advisors to the Holy Father. In any case, his prophecies and messages are held in high esteem in some circles. But I wouldn't get too excited. He also stated a third world war would take place and at the same time most of the world would be hit by natural disasters and devastated. All of this was to be finished by 1994. John Paul was also to die in 1994, and Biernacki claims the Antichrist was born in the Middle East in the year 1977, an incarnate angel. He also stated that if the Queen of England did not return to the faith, she will soon find that she has become completely paralyzed. The Soviets will become extinct, he added. Bishop Hnilica states our salvation is hinged on saving Russia.

And so we have a veritable cadre of modern day prophets, messengers, and mystics, some undoubtedly very authentic, many others just well intentioned, some emotionally unstable, and some just being deceived by that age old angel of light and father of lies. And without question, there is the apparent reality that Our Lady and Her Son are indeed desperately trying to reach mankind with warnings and messages for a self-destructing world. The only question now is, which is which?

That should give us a much greater respect for the position of the Church in the matter of private revelation. It literally verifies the wisdom of the Church in "taking her time" to act on matters of private revelation (even though the delay with Fatima might have been a little much). She knows it is not a case of requiring anyone to believe in such-

and-such apparitions. And the possible negative effects of false ones are enormous.

As noted throughout this book, even those that seem credible, or that even have received Church endorsement have critics, and some, critics with some pretty impressive arguments. We recently published a book regarding the apparitions at Cuapa, Nicaragua. The decision to publish it was based on approval from the Bishops there, the fact that the visionary entered the seminary and became a priest, and the lack of confusion and dissension regarding the apparitions. On the other hand, consider other seemingly authentic sites that have produced divisions, critics and supporters. Bishop Zanic enthusiastically opposed Medjugorje. Bishop Franic enthusiastically supported it. Akita (Japan) has its critics, principally because of its constant chastisement theme. Damascus (visionary, Mirna) supposedly was endorsed by a number of faiths but has found all kinds of difficulties.

Maria Esperanza (Betania) is strongly supported and was approved by the local bishop there. Critics of Betania cite a bishop whose investigative commission was composed of only himself, and dissatisfaction with certain messages, prophecies, and activities of the seer. One report stated that a certain Cardinal in the Church, personally acquainted with the seer, was openly opposed to her. Supporters point to numerous signs and wonders, the rose phenomena (also used by critics), and a Eucharistic miracle and various healings. Which is correct? In some cases, these debates and tests of authenticity carry over from one century to the next. Maria Valtorta (*Poem of the Man God*), Mary of Agreda, and Luisa Piccarreta (the Divine Will) are but three examples. The work of Satan to destroy authentic touches provided from Heaven? Or could it be the work of Satan to manufacture a few false ones of his own?

There does appear to be great hope and some clear self aids in the evaluation of all of this, but it might help to first identify a few more of the problem areas to get a clearer picture of the under-the-surface confusion that exists.

Bad Prophecy and Theology

Peter tells us (*2 Peter*, Chapter 2), about false teachers, past and future. Prophets and visions abound in Scripture. All of them weren't right either. Does that invalidate the Bible?

Then why should it invalidate any current claimed vision-ary in America, or wherever? St. Paul and the Apostles pro-vided many references about the "return of the Lord" in their lifetime. They missed by almost two thousand years—so far. Jonah preached the certain destruction of Nineveh. It wasn't. Some very famous saints and doctors of the Church have pulled some *faux-pas*. All of that just provides more reason for the need of heavy duty discernment.

Today there also appears to be a problem with many prophecies that didn't materialize as scheduled. This is true concerning a number of topics, and many claimed visionaries are involved, or are in conflict with one another. Those topics are: natural disasters, the anti-christ appearing, the chastisement, the death of the Pope, the split in the Church. Sometimes these errors are explained away as "being delayed because of the volume of prayers." This apparently means that a visionary giving prophecy can NEVER be wrong; it can always be delayed or miti-gated because of our responses. But that becomes pretty hard to accept when you read so many different messages that emphatically state that the apostasy, the chastisement, the three days of darkness, the return of the Lord, the whole thing is coming down right now. Now is the time, His hand cannot be stayed, and the reason for it all is our total lack of prayer and conversion. Then comes a message that says it has all been held back because of our prayer and conversion.

In reading Scripture it sometimes seems like most of the Old Testament was steeped in chastisement. There were all kinds of prophets bringing news to the people, and much of it bad. The just God seemed to be laying some heavy hits on His people. It is hard to imagine the world then could have been any more evil than it is now. The emergence of the Incarnation of the Word, the Messiah, seemed to change all of that for awhile and the "Good News" was that of love, humility, forgiveness, hope and redemption. But even the Lord laid out some bad news as well:

> *Nation will rise against nation, one kingdom against another. There will be famine and pestilence and earthquakes in diverse places (Matt. 24:7-8).*
> *Many will falter then, betraying and hating one*

another. False prophets will rise in great numbers to
mislead many. Because of the increase of evil, the
love of most will grow cold (Matt. 24:10-14).
  There will be signs in the sun, the moon and the
stars. On the earth, nations will be in anguish, dis-
traught at the roaring of the sea and the waves. Men
will die of fright in anticipation of what is coming
upon the earth. The powers in the heavens will be
shaken. After that, men will see the Son of Man com-
ing on a cloud with great power and glory (Luke
21:25-27).

Those are some pretty heavy words and sure fit where we
are and what we need right now. Other prophets came on
the scene as well, and presented us with additional insight
into this realm of chastisement. Unfortunately, not all have
been very accurate and this includes some of the big names
from the "Hall of Fame" of the Catholic Church. Today's
prophets seem to have an even worse record. Bad theology
has also been added to the list, not just prophecy.

Some visionaries today provide us with messages that say
"this is to be added to public revelation." I believe that is a
definite no-no. Or they tell us of new doctrines, changes in
Church liturgies and practices, threats and demands from
God, or a whole bunch of new books Our Lady wants published. Bad theology today is a many headed monster. That
is particularly evident from materials provided by visionaries in California, in the southern Ohio/northern Kentucky
area, Conyers, Georgia and Bella Vista, Arkansas. But it is
called "private revelation" so no Imprimatur is required for
the books (and none sought). For example, Vassula, among
many other questionable messages, provided one that said
Jesus says "to get rid of your liturgies." Given her doubtful
statements concerning "unity" and the World Council of
Churches, saying we are supposed to give up our liturgy is
probably suspect.

Much of it is far more subtle than that. It can come excel-
lently packaged and makes it very difficult to discern. Such
might be the case with the **"Jesus, King of All Nations"**
booklet. It is loaded with all kinds of promises, devotions,
litanies, novenas, medals, prayers, and more promises. And

that's fine. The Lord can certainly do whatever He wants, without our permission—certainly not mine. But I can list a number of questions that have surfaced regarding this devotion as an example of discernment needs.

In any case the JKAN materials have created a rather extensive file of people who question or doubt. Regular calls for money may be part of the problem, but questionable theology seems to be also. The booklet received a *"Nihil Obstat,"* under some questionable process. It was obtained from a bishop in Puerto Rico. Bishops in the area where this material originates did not endorse it (such as in Connecticut, Vermont, and Virginia). The Executive Director for the Secretariat for Doctrine and Pastoral Practices (*National Conference of Catholic Bishops*) evidently didn't support it either, nor did the *Fatima Family Apostolate Magazine*. A number of locations supposedly cancelled JKAN programs, and one report had it that the large image of JKAN was removed from the National Shrine of the Immaculate Conception in Washington, D.C. Another says that the bishops in Mexico were upset that this movement was being linked to and promoted with the Missionary Image of "Our Lady of Guadalupe." In any case, such items are cause for reflection in the discernment process.

This devotion to JKAN stems from a couple of ladies in the Falls Church, Virginia area. It is claimed it is the result of apparitions from Jesus to His "servants," which produced the "Jesus King of All Nations" booklet, medal, messages and new devotional materials. They seem to be a copycat of other messages and devotions claimed by other seers. For example, it is a strong endorsement of the CoRedemptrix-Mediatrix of All Graces program, as well as Fatima, and Sr. Faustina and the Divine Mercy format. In fact, the booklet states that Jesus stated this is to be used in conjunction with the Sr. Faustina materials. There seems to be concern over the endless list of promises Jesus has added through these messages. If you partake in all of the devotions, novenas, litanies, etc. as shown, you almost have your eternal salvation guaranteed, and, Jesus will personally appear to you before you die. There is a special blessing included which you can give to others along with certain prayers to be said in the process, which means you can become the instrument of giving special graces. Jesus also **demanded** that the Church proclaim the dogma of Mary-Mediatrix, and stated *"only then will I establish My Reign on earth."* There also seems to be some concern about that title of "King of All Nations." Some equated it with the antichrist's title and position of king of all nations, or with an antichrist who is to rule the "United Nations" organization, hence, the entire world. They question whether it opposes a title of Jesus already established by the Church, **Christ the King.** We need to simply see all of this as an example of the confusion that has built up in the Marian Movement over the past five years. A couple other examples are shown in the appendix of this book.

Following are additional message segments from American visionaries that you may want to question. Again, there is no intent here to dishonor any visionary by name, it is simply a case of providing some excerpts from existing messages to identify a possible need for discernment on the part of those reading them. They are presented as messages from Our Lord or Our Lady and a selection is as follows:

—*We are in the last hours . . . the earthquake on the West coast will be devastating* (Aug. '92).
—*The last three months of 1992 will be the total destruction of America. The land shall be ravaged.*
—*The earth will split in half.*
—*The great earthquake is not even months away* (May. '92).
—*A great war is coming. A great punishment is coming for California.*
—*Never has your continent seen such destruction. It will be worse than the civil war* (May '92).
—*Pray intensely through the night, this is the last night you have . . . the hour has come . . . no more can be done* (May '92).
—*Antichrist has come . . . he wears human form and convinces all to whom he speaks. . . . I have shown you the face of Antichrist.*
—*I solemnly tell you, the moment of great darkness has come* (July '91).
—*At Bayside I have given you these warnings. And at*

Necedah I have given you these warnings. Now at this time throughout this world I give you this warning America.

—*The time is not far away, my children. It is less than two years when he* (the Pope) *shall flee Rome only to return again to meet and embrace martyrdom for Holy Mother church. Very soon will be seen in the nations of Italy, Spain, and France, rivalry within the streets, great social and political unrest* (Given in 1990).

—*I tell you the conflict in the Persian Gulf shall not be short . . . Many nations shall wage war. From the smoke of this war shall rise the antichrist. He is here* (Jan. '91).

—*The economy of the world shall collapse in a very short time* (Jan. '91).

—*I do solemnly tell you that in the following months of this year* (Aug. '92) *you shall experience many signs which shall lead your world into total collapse. Tremendous earthquakes shall devastate, particularly in this country . . . the economy will collapse . . . the land shall be ravaged.*

—*The martyrdom of Pope John Paul II is imminent* (June '92).

—*The time for the great schism is here* (May '91).

—*Pray for the Pope who will soon be silenced* (Jan. '91).

—*War will come, brutal, swift, changing the earth forever . . . attempts made to bring peace to the Persian Gulf are maneuvers by Satan's legions . . . the antichrist walks the earth and has come to a position of great power . . . Satan's legions will strike out even silencing the holy voice of the Vicar of Christ . . . chaos shall reign.* (Gulf War)

—*Do not let anyone tell you that this war will be over and peace will reign.* (Persian Gulf). *It is the chastisement. . . . This war shall spread to other lands. . . . Terrorism shall be the rule soon and no one shall be safe. Life as it has been lived in this century shall pass away* (Jan. '91).

A number of messages over the past five years give much detail regarding abortion being the reason to trigger the chastisement. There are also many messages alluding to the great schism in the Church and the imminent state of apostasy. Several messages stated the prediction of the end of the Persian Gulf war, as given by Our Lord.

Much of this information was common knowledge in that it has been before us for some time. The evil of abortion has been with us for over twenty years and few doubt that it calls out for vengeance from the Lord. The Church is in somewhat of a crisis and for those of us who have been involved, it is not difficult to see the creation of the "American Catholic Church." Those two points alone are enough reason for the chastisement to come and I for one, think it will. But when?

Predicting the end of the Persian Gulf war didn't require any visionaries. Anyone with a television set, anywhere in the world, who watched the first war ever fought and reported via television could have predicted the end within a few days. Are all the above prophecies wrong? Are some of them? Who am I to say. Didn't St. Peter tell us that God is not on the same calendar or time that we are:

In the Lord's eyes, one day is as a thousand years and a thousand years are as a day. (2 Ptr. 3:8)

Why not just let God be God?

Spiritual Entertainment

That is a term I borrowed from Michael Brown in a small article he did regarding discernment. Michael's professionalism obviously shows through in his work, not only in the depth of his journalism but in his spirituality as well. He mentioned spiritual entertainment as a possible malaise of our age of supernatural phenomena. It is a point well taken. Message books, and more books—and video and audio cassettes. Too many with too much sensationalism included. Is a certain portion of it just spiritual entertainment? If it is, it becomes a major concern because there are too many thousands of people who have taken that entertainment to heart. Their faith may be at stake.

St. Teresa of Avila, a Doctor of the Church, has left us volumes on the spiritual life. Included is much data on private revelations and apparitions. Among these admonishments, she gave us several cautions on locutions, stating that if they treat of some weighty (theological) matter in which we are called to act, or if they concern any third person by name, or address the personal situations of a third person, we should be extremely cautious. Many of the messages today fall into these categories. The theology is extremely suspect and the people involved, including some priests, do not seem to want any Chancery offices looking into that theology. More importantly, the messages often involve other parties—third or fourth parties—other claimed seers or organizations, publishers, parishes, liturgical practices, etc.

I wonder if anyone else gets the feeling that some messages are being presented as being more important than the words of Scripture? There also seems to be a need to read between the lines on some of those messages that appear like Our Lady is admonishing anyone who would doubt any of her alleged messengers. We have seen this on a worldwide basis, where you can interpret the message as saying "you better believe this or else." Does that mean we shouldn't question messages like:

— *You have a best-seller here* (Jesus to one visionary regarding the planned message book).
— *My Mother, part of the Holy Trinity of God* (Fourth person of the Trinity?)
— *I do not appear like this anywhere else on earth. No where are my graces being poured forth like they are here.*
— *Pope John Paul will be gone before 1993.*

Mercy

The subject of mercy is also a very major concern in so many messages today. Many seers tell us God's mercy has come to an end. He is sick and tired of us and our unfaithfulness (not that He doesn't have good reason to be). Others keep preaching that Gospel message of love and forgiveness. Personally, I suggest you question any message that speaks of the end of God's mercy.

— *Mankind shall receive no further mercy or warning.*
— *Mercy is everlasting when it comes from the Father.*
— *Soon my Father's mercy will end.*

The above three examples of different views of mercy are only three of three hundred examples that we could list here. Am I, (or you), to believe that this same Jesus who hung in terrible pain on a cross, after suffering the torment of scourging and being crowned with thorns; this same Jesus who carried the instrument of His death to the crucifixion site, who then, from that cross prayed: *"Father forgive them, they know not what they do";* is the same Jesus who is now saying: "That's it! No more mercy!" I doubt it. If that is true, then He died for nothing, and we have no more possible hope. It's all over.

The writings of Sr. Faustina, at least in my opinion, should be at the top of our reading list. Evidently the Pope thinks so as well as he continues with the march to sainthood for this incredible nun. The **Divine Mercy**, as detailed in her diary, gives the laity substantial confirmation of all the elements of our faith and the truths of the Gospels. In the past ten years, the **Chaplet of Divine Mercy** has become almost as popular as the Rosary. The little *"Devotion to Divine Mercy"* booklet (highly recommended), is an integral part of it all. It basically says you can make it by just loving Jesus, living His words, and honoring His Mother. If there is any "for sure hope" for this world, it is the reality of **Divine Mercy,** not the end of it.

A Pope Says . . .

In books dealing with private revelation today, it is "good hype" to quote the claimed words of Pope Urban VIII who supposedly stated it is better to believe than to not believe—even if the claimed apparitions turn out to be proved false. What you never see in the same books are other Church leaders who stated the opposite. For example, Pope Leo X published a Bull prohibiting public prophecies by preachers as a result of over-zealous activity in the prophecy business. In 1872, as the result of a vast infusion of apparitions and prophecies, Pius IX openly criticized them adding: "I think that they are the fruit of the imagination." Pope Benedict XIII, at the close of the great western schism (1420), was deposed. The story goes that he had relied on a vision from an Abbot who told him what the future would bring. Benedict supposedly based his decisions on this vision and it cost him his position on the pulpit.

Regarding the previously referenced support of any claimed apparitions as credited to Pope Urban VIII, which I have not been able to verify, there is finally, the words of another occupant of the Chair of Peter. Benedict XIV came down quite hard on visionaries of his day. As stated previously in this book, he stressed that private revelation, "although approved of, ought not to, and cannot receive from us any assent of Catholic, but only human faith."

And as noted earlier, the Holy See has consistently upheld this position and it has also been specifically stated in the Vatican II documents and in the New Catechism. Thus has the Church spoken.

What if it's Wrong?

And any private revelation could be wrong. It was noted earlier in this chapter how the New Age Movement has jumped on board. Other movements and faiths have as well. Suddenly it seems to becoming intermingled.

There is something here we all really need to concentrate on, and it is indeed a reality. Satan is a counterfeit. He duplicates and counterfeits absolutely everything. The occult has its own mass, its own baptism, its own bible. For every beatitude there is an opposite evil. Also with apparitions and visions. Satan even made it into the Bible.

As we have repeatedly noted, the New Age Movement is part of that counterfeit religion—complete with false visionaries and messages, complete with its own hierarchy of supernatural masters, complete with its own array of miracles and psychics. More and more messages become more and more deceptive—much true teaching. As we have previously noted, Satan will gladly give you 95% light if he can also get you to accept 5% darkness.

There are New Age restaurants, churches, doctors and health centers, magazines and radio and TV programs. Channelers are becoming wealthy. So are New Age publishers. Bantam Books increased their New Age line ten times in the past decade. Ruth Norman, a New Age guru and author has over one-half million subscribers to her newsletter. Shirley MacLaine's book, *Out On a Limb*, sold millions of copies. In 1986 there were reportedly 2,400 New Age bookshops in the United States. In the mid-nineties there are over 5,000. *Psychic Guide* and *New Age Magazine*, New Age publications, have hundreds of thousands of subscribers. There are even psychic training schools.

The good news is that there is a tremendous supernatural

renewal underway, a great spiritual hunger. The bad news is that the wrong spirit—or at least the wrong motives—are often behind it. Please beware of the reality of that. Some examples would be as follows:

Channelers, mediums, pendants, crystals, astrology and a number of other New Age practices are specifically identified in the Scriptures, and are forbidden. Read Chapters 17 and 18 of the book of *Deuteronomy* as just one of many Biblical confirmations.

A second example is the diversion created by what seem like true messages. They can tickle our ears, command our attention, captivate our imaginations, or push us to read other seemingly recommended books. What does this accomplish? It steers us away from reading the Bible, or perhaps the New Catechism.

A third example is what we are all facing today, a growing and spreading plague of contemporary communications.

Electronic Visionaries and Theologians?

Listing the pluses of this new electronic communications age is a major task. It would become a very lengthy list indeed. Advancements galore and a whole new concept of education as well as communication.

The evil also is becoming very apparent, and it is far more than just pornography. The Internet! Cyberspace! The information superhighway! Your own web page. Instant contact with all that is happening in the spiritual realm. That certainly can't be labeled as evil unto itself. But there is a need for all of us to be aware, to be discerning.

Any claimed visionary today, Catholic or otherwise, or anyone who wishes to pass themselves off as mystics has access to the Internet, access to millions of people worldwide. And who is monitoring those messages, approving the doctrinal aspect of the messages being conveyed? Who is to prevent you or I from advancing our own brand of theologies and beliefs?

Much of this type of material is also available through the "chat room" concept of electronic communications. Everyone can find his or her place there, express their views of religious belief, and/or relate their experiences with the supernatural messengers they have been in contact with. The pluses are indeed enormous. So are the negatives.

Could the testing of visionaries be an additional example? Why not? If Satan can duplicate and counterfeit everything, could he also produce false results to testing procedures? He can bend spoons, lift tables, create possessions, trauma, even death. He can work miracles, produce phenomena of all kinds. Why can't he do tricks with electrical and electronic gadgets? I would think he can—and has.

Visionaries (including Medjugorje) get tested and all kinds of data is recorded and presented as authenticating so and so. Nancy Fowler in Georgia, and Barbara Matthias in California, for example, had all kinds of tests. Results are based on delta waves, radiation (gamma waves), energy concentrations, electrical stimulation, and the such, produced by a vast array of technical apparatus. Why can't all of that be true? Obviously it can, and it is very impressive. On the other hand, New Age gurus and occultists can do much of the same. Lourdes and Fatima had to find approval without any tests.

Perhaps it comes down to our being willing to accept that something can be wrong in the area of private revelation, to be more discerning in our acceptance, and to do something about it when the Holy Spirit is giving us those little, disconcerting signs that something is not for real.

If there is an immediate need for us to correct a flaw in the process (and there are several such needs), it may be to recognize and adjust accordingly when private revelation is wrong. At times it seems we simply brush off events, or messages, or Church positions that don't fit our needs or desires and concentrate only on what we want to see or hear. It is truly amazing how easy it is for us to **not** see or hear something we do not want to see or hear. Only the "acceptable" portion of the message is apparent to our eyes or ears. It even reaches the point where we are able to dismiss major aspects that did not pan out or that were ruled against by the Church (the disapproved apparitions at Necedah and Bayside to cite two instances).

At Pescara, Italy, a young priest, Don Vicenzo, became involved in pilgrimages to Medjugorje. In the process he became a follower of a claimed visionary named Maria Antonina Fioriti who became very vocal as well as public in her claims. She announced a great miracle to occur on February 28, 1988:

A sign in the sun as at Fatima by day. Another in the night sky, around midnight.

Supported by Fr. Vicenzo, a great promotion was undertaken for the coming event. Over one hundred thousand people assembled along with the press and television. The result was only great disillusion. Nothing happened. To his credit, Fr. Vicenzo recognized his error and left for a long retreat in a monastery.

A similar event took place in the United States, but with some interesting connections. In early March of 1993, a major message was distributed to Marian organizations all over the country, mostly by fax. It came from Kettle River, Minnesota, and announced that Our Lady would be appearing there on Easter Sunday at 3:00 p.m. The event was to be a "miracle greater than any time in the history of Our Blessed Mother's appearances." Thousands were to see her.

They didn't.

Obviously, there was much disappointment that the event did not come off as planned, but deflated enthusiasm did not last long. People regrouped and carried on, off to another apparition site somewhere else. Interestingly, it did provide a phenomenon of another kind. Almost immediately with the announcement of March 19, 1993, there were other seers who confirmed the event with messages of their own, and still others who received messages that they were indeed to go there to be part of the great event.

That is something that you might wish to check into. It has become quite common and has some disturbing elements intertwined. What sometimes seems to be happening is that when any major supernatural phenomenon is announced, many other visionaries/locutionists immediately endorse it or confirm it. It's like you can't afford not to be involved in the festivities. For example, check the time frame of the release of the new promotion for the proposed new Marian Dogma and the book produced by Dr. Mark Miravalle *(Mediatrix-Coredemptrix-Advocate)*. Then check other messengers involved in private revelation to determine if any suddenly are promoting the same title and the same message. Such is the case as well with the "Jesus King of All Nations" booklet and devotion.

Some of that may be a positive confirmation as well. Then again, it may not. It is worth your effort to find out.

You often see or hear this "proof" of the authenticity of all these messages: "This must be right because all of the visionaries are saying the same thing. All the messages are the same."

No, not all.

Some are just copied.

Studying thirty or forty message books can become one very depressing and tedious undertaking. But you can uncover a number of things that might make you want to question certain messages, and messengers. You might find:

- They suddenly seem to copy each other (as needed).
- They confirm each other on a major event, or a major prophecy (often wrong).
- They need to endorse, or be part of, any new devotion, proposed dogma, or highly publicized conference or pilgrimage.
- And finally, you might want to question why it seems that when and if they are not part of it all, they seem to get messages that say there are many false visionaries and messages around today.

But as far as all the messages being the same? As quoted elsewhere in this book, by example, that is not always so. Unity is supposedly endorsed by all seers. Fr. Gobbi evidently doesn't accept that, and Josyp Terelya, in his new book, wails against Jews and Russians and states that "ecumenism is an unforgivable sin." Still others produce messages that state the world is full of false seers hindering unity.

Medjugorje is generally accepted as the apparition site that has kick-started all of this private revelation interest. And, most of the current messengers of heavenly visitations have been to Medjugorje. Naturally, then, the critics of Medjugorje are quick to point out that it is just the launching pad for all of this.

Interestingly, the more you check into it and study the messages, the more you find the opposite is true. Medjugorje begins to stand out more and more like a lighthouse to a ship in a stormy sea. Following are a few of the Medjugorje messages from Our Lady. Contrast these words with other messages you have read elsewhere in this book.

To some, all is in Mary's hands. To some, she is the **only** refuge. In 1983, at Medjugorje, she stated:

I am not able to cure you. God alone can cure you. Pray. I will pray with you. I am not God. I need your prayers and your sacrifices to help me....You do not need a sign; you yourselves must be a sign.

August 12, 1984

The only attitude of the Christian toward the future is hope of salvation. Those who think only of wars, evil, punishment, do not do well. If you think of evil, punishment, wars, you are on the road to meeting them. Your responsibility is to accept Divine peace, live it and spread it.

October 7, 1981

Question: Is there, outside of Jesus, other intermediaries between God and man, and what is their role?

Answer: *There is only one mediator between God and man, and it is Jesus Christ.*

July 12, 1982

Question: Will there be a third world war?

Answer: *The third world war will not take place.*

September 4, 1982

Regarding a question of should we pray to Mary or Jesus?

Jesus prefers that you address yourselves directly to Him rather than through an intermediary. In the meantime, if you wish to give yourselves completely to God and if you wish that I be your protector, then confide to me all your intentions ...

August 31, 1982

Concerning Mary's role in dispensing grace, she responded:

*I do **not** dispose all graces. I receive from God what I obtain through prayer. God has placed His complete trust in me ...*

The great sign has been granted. It will appear independently of the conversion of the people.

There is one other comparison that needs to be made in attempting to use Medjugorje as a gauge or standard for some of the claimed messages we have been receiving elsewhere over the past ten years. And it's not one message. It's years and years worth. The **Lady** has produced thousands of messages at Medjugorje that all project the same needs, the same requests, the same guidelines—even to the point that some people think they are too repetitive, too mundane. She keeps telling us to *pray, pray, pray.* Prayer and fasting is always there. So is the word "conversion." What is not there are threats, and punishment, and purifications and chastisement. She doesn't use the words "end times," or how we are all going to die in these imminent disasters. She speaks of hope, and peace—always peace—and consecrating our lives to Jesus, and also to her Immaculate Heart.

And there is one other element that is always there in fifteen years of messages. Maybe it's why she chose Medjugorje to begin with, with its peasant lifestyle, and lack of "contemporary" niceties.

She keeps telling us to simplify our lives. Simplifying lifestyles seems to be her way to achieve the prayer, fasting, conversion, etc. that she requests of us. *Matthew* 6:24-34 was specifically mentioned early on in her messages. Maybe we need to study it. It's about that same topic: **Simplify your life.**

She reminds us we are on pilgrimage here—not to Medjugorje, but to Heaven. This is only temporary and not really important anyway. Get the confusion out of your life. Get the stress out, the bitterness, the darkness. Get God in! Slow down! Simplify!

Compare that to some of the sensationalism, the stressful, gloom and doom warnings you read today. Compare that to all of this—more books, more videos, more devotions and chaplets and novenas and pilgrimages and conferences and searches for more signs and wonders.

At this point it is necessary to mention the fact that the events at Medjugorje are under scrutiny as well. It has always been opposed by various elements of the Church Hierarchy, while on the other hand, endorsed by other elements, apparently including the Pope. Again this summer (1996), a press release surfaced stating that official pilgrimages to Medjugorje were not acceptable. The key word here is "official," meaning those that are authorized, organized or openly endorsed and participated in by the ordainted Church. Obviously, it is an attempt (and rightly so) to eliminate the perception that the Church is openly promoting Medjugorje prior to any final ruling on the apparitions.

And there have been other questions as well. There always has been at apparition sites. There always will be. That is why it is identified as "private" revelation. It is necessary to pray for a peaceful and beneficial solution to the Medjugorje events. Such has been the influence of Medjugorje on the lives of millions. But for the same reasons, it has to be found as "worthy of belief." Nonetheless the messages coming from this remote spot of the world have left little room for criticism. They seem to be a reflection of Church and Biblical teaching, regardless of personal feelings toward the seers. It will be these same seers, along with the merit of the messages and the physical and spiritual healings that can be measured at Medjugorje, that will determine whether they are worthy of belief. To date, there seems to be little to debate regarding the messages the Madonna seems to be giving there. I think she's really saying, let God be God.

Isn't it amazing how today we have sometimes responded to her constant requests to simplify our lives? We come up with a chain of fax machines so that you will be sure to get the vital message when it happens. You can buy into a computer hook-up, almost like a franchise, to make certain you will be informed. Phone networks were tried. All kinds of newsletters, phone chains. Sell this, store that. Move to "safe havens," regardless of your job or your family or your parish or school. Carry this scapular. Wear this medal. Say this prayer—maybe even swallow it. You must read these books. If you don't go to Conyers, your country is in big trouble.

She never told anybody to write books at Medjugorje, or make films, or produce medals or install computer hook-ups or phone chains, or go to this shrine or that. She said **simplify your life.** Convert back to Jesus. **Humility** seemed to be a part of it all, not **pride.** She spoke so often of peace and love and giving, not of our egos.

Wow! What a contrast. Have we missed the boat somehow here? Are we still trying to out-fox the Lord, beat the chastisement, buy our way into Heaven by collecting message books, medals, rosaries that turned gold, magic photos, and new devotions?

And finally there is one other very important message that Our Lady reportedly gave at Medjugorje. It was early on in the apparitions and a famous doctor from Italy, who had produced a film and two very inspirational books on the events, was there for a specific apparition. He asked one of the visionaries to ask Our Lady what she thought of the books. The reported response was:

> *Tell him the world has enough books and films. What the world needs is more prayer.*

I think of that often—every time we consider doing another book regarding Medjugorje, or any other book dealing with private revelation. I certainly thought about it for a long while before I did this one. There seems to be so much truth to that claimed response from the Virgin. And what a contrast to some of the crazy messages coming from alleged visionaries in the U.S.

The Lord God never seemed to need any books, or the need to rely on mass communications to get His message across. Technology was never given as the ultimate answer. In fact He only needed one book. It's titled **The Bible.** And Jesus? He never wrote any. Nor did He ask His disciples to write any. Neither did Mary—that the Church has confirmed. She always has been satisfied with being that quiet, humble woman of the New Testament, Mother of the Redeemer, and content to be in the background, reflecting a radiance and holiness, and at the same time a total submission to the will of God.

Now, according to the Batavia visionary and "Our Lady of Light," she makes appearances holding "her books" in the air. That seems an insult.

In keeping with the Madonna's role in the Bible, the documents of Vatican II, and the traditions and teachings of the

Church over the centuries, we have always had a view of Mary as only **leading to Jesus.** She claims nothing for herself, seeks no glory of her own, nor any position of authority or prominence. She comes only to call her children back to the Redeemer, Her Son. She comes only on behalf of the Lord. And, with many claimed apparitions today, she fits that exact mold, that same image.

But we also get some where she comes proclaiming *my books, my ministries, my house, my farm, my shrine, my Church, my priests.* She comes giving names and titles to ministries and books, who is in charge of what, who can and can't. The final outrage in the *"Personal Revelations of Our Lady of Light"* books appeared in the final edition where Our Lady actually does a "dedication page" at the start of the book along with the standard acknowledgment page of: "I would like to thank so and so, etc."

Dear Lady, what are we doing to you? You have indeed become big business, and also heavily commercialized. But how could anyone really believe that is you when reading that? Our intentions might indeed be good, our enthusiasm high, but how much of the reality of your appearances are we now fabricating ourselves? And for what reason?

And what about the author of this book? What of Bill Reck and this apostolate? Have I ever been wrong? You must be kidding! I know my sin history, just as you know yours. I bet mine is longer—and larger. There is no claim of righteousness here. My work is not being offered as some kind of noble effort. There is only one noble effort to be concerned with, only one righteous apostolate—and that is the Marian Movement—Our Lady's Apostolate. That is what we must safeguard, what we must defend. It is vital to the Church.

Sure, I've made mistakes with The Riehle Foundation and/or Faith Publishing Company. I guess only time will tell if, or how many, I made with this book. A good example to show the need for discernment, while at the same time trying to determine what to do, or not do, with certain books, is the fourth volume of the book, *I Am Your Jesus Of Mercy.* We didn't publish it. We didn't publish it because we felt too many of the messages involved were strictly of a personal nature, that the style and delivery was changing throughout, and that the vocabulary changing from page to page indicated that it was not the same person who authored it throughout. I also found that some material in that series of books could have come from elsewhere. For example, one particular lesson was almost word for word from a certain page in the book, *The Imitation of Christ.* A further check and study of other new aspects of the events in Scottsdale, particularly regarding specific persons, was reason for not publishing additional message books or additional books by Fr. Robert Faricy and Fr. Renè Laurentin without the bishop's endorsement.

Does that mean I no longer believe in the *I Am Your Jesus Of Mercy* books we did publish? No it doesn't. If we didn't believe in them, I would pull them off of the market. We have distributed over 650,000 copies of those books and have received, literally, thousands of letters of testimonial in their behalf. Tremendous letters! And "thousands of letters" is not a figure of speech. It really is thousands and thousands. In contrast, we received eight to ten opposed to the books. Additionally, profit was not a factor.

My absolute right to be wrong caused us to once pull a book off the market the very day it came out because of information I received, and that I should have known in the first place. Certain persons I relied upon (not affiliated with our apostolate) proved to be an opposing force, perhaps not even a good force.

Sure, I can be as wrong or as guilty as anyone else. And you can rest assured that Satan will have a turn at all of us involved in Our Lady's work and Our Lord's Church, and that certainly includes visionaries and locutionists, or those who think they are or want to be. But Our Lady's work is vital to the Mystical Body of Christ, and it **must be protected,** regardless of the cost.

Personally, I do not believe there are any private revelations that do not include some area of question and the cited examples of some of the difficulties of past saints imply as much. Still, the increase of supernatural manifestations of the past ten years has generated the danger of a new cult whose interest in the latest message of so and so, or the latest prophecy of chastisement is taking precedence over all other matters, including the needs of the Church.

It was interesting to read, a few years ago, of the church in

Korea that had a special insight of the coming rapture and end times, and on a given date the congregation sold all of their property, quit their jobs and marched out to the countryside to await the event. Then, when the heavenly bus didn't come by, the community was left with all these unemployed and homeless people. Are some of us also waiting for a bus?

Billions, literally billions of people have lived on this earth prior to you and me. Do you know how many made it out of this world alive? That's right, so I guess the bottom line is that you and I are going to die. Ultimately, it really doesn't matter how, or when, or where. The only thing that is important is the condition of our souls. So that is the only thing we need to be concerned about. The rest of it is out of our hands—and everybody else's. Only HE has the answer.

This Book Is Too Negative!

I'm sure that will be the response of some readers. But perhaps there is a need to re-evaluate a little here before we go on. Please consider that what is being presented to you here is simply a compilation of many messages and statements from thousands of pages of material as reported by many, many claimed visionaries. It is offered here as a study, an evaluation, a sampling, to show where the pitfalls occur, where Satan lurks.

Unfortunately, what seems to come down at times is that any message from any claimed visionary, regardless of how sensational it is, or how much gloom and doom and chastisement it contains, is acceptable reading (or worthy of belief perhaps). Names of the visionaries/locutionists are often openly revealed along with the apparition site and when the next message will be given. Criticism of the Church or liturgical practices seem acceptable, as well as questionable theology. Benefitting economically is OK, and potential harm to a reader's emotional or spiritual well being is considered part of the territory. That is how it now appears.

However, prepare to be castigated if you dare take the other side. We claim we are allowed to believe in any private revelation, but it is considered slander if you say you don't believe in so and so. Can it eventually come to the point where you feel an obligation to believe all private revelation, are not permitted to oppose any seer, and are personally opposing the Blessed Virgin Mary or Her Son if you do so?

Well, hogwash.

It is probably time for many people to at least **hear** the other side—that not all of this private revelation is authentic and perhaps should be avoided. At the least, there should be an opportunity to evaluate the situation and I don't know how you do that without identifying the vision and/or the material involved. There has certainly been little hesitation from those who wish you to support it. Maybe you need to carefully evaluate the other side. If that is negative, so be it.

These are very exciting times. Very troubled times, and evidently a time when many people are bringing us some startling news from supernatural visits. It is happening worldwide. With it comes responsibility and a need to discern. There is a possibility that the aspect of discernment has been lacking, so all of these previous pages have been presented to show examples and past experiences of others relating to apparitions, and also the thoughts of some of our Church leaders.

In the final analysis, it will never be just a mystic that will save your soul. Neither can I. So maybe we need to concentrate more on who can. Let God be God.

CHAPTER 5

The Positive Side

She's real. Like Her Son is real. Like His death, Resurrection and Ascension are real. Like His Sacraments are real.

She came on the scene as the "New Eve," the "New Ark of the Covenant," to prepare a fallen world for its promised Savior. She's been doing the same thing ever since. She's been the object of great devotion (and great ridicule) for centuries. Next to her Son, she leads the world in books, paintings, sculpture, hymns, and man-made structures produced in her honor. She was named "Mother" for all mankind. Her following goes all the way back to the coming of the Messiah and includes billions of people over the centuries.

And, she has responded. She was there keeping the emerging Church together, mothering eleven anxious apostles while they awaited the promised Paraclete. She apparently was the inspiration needed for the Church to grow, as evidenced by the writings of the early Church fathers, and the cathedrals and works of art dedicated to her in the first years. She was at the forefront of the first councils, the object of initial heresies, the point of defense in doctrines and dogmas. She was the object of some of the works of the masters, like Michelangelo, and honored repeatedly by Popes. She has come in times of special need to produce countless miracles and unexplainable phenomena. She was guiding the Church at the battle of Lepanato in 1571, and through the trying period of the Reformation and the Renaissance. She gave us sacramentals that have endured for centuries, the scapular, the Rosary, medals such as the Miraculous Medal. Her appearances to Catherine Laboure were followed by LaSalette and Lourdes, merely several examples of many apparitions that have been there from the start, and that are still occurring today. They have produced countless prophecies, doctrines, devotions, conversions, and healings. They have been the cement that has kept the Church together through particularly difficult times, and for many centuries.

There are many excellent books that detail the history of Mary and her role in the Church. A number of them are mentioned throughout this book. Suffice it to say that she is as important, and permanent to the Church, as the sun is to the earth, as air is to our life.

Let's just concentrate on this century. It is our century, and a century of the greatest advancements, and the greatest self-destruction the world has ever known. Here again, Mary, often through private revelation, is right there in the middle of it all. You might not want to believe in the private revelation, but you still can't remove her from the history of this century—already established or about to be.

In 1917 chaos ruled in much of the world. While the industrial revolution was bringing great change to societies in general, the economy of many countries was in shambles, and discontent was wide-spread . . . most notably in Russia where revolt was underway. The evil of Communism was about to rear its ugly head. World War I was raging, causing great loss of life and untold destruction. Life in Portugal was no better, and there, the Church was considered the enemy.

And she came. The location was a tiny village called **Fatima**.

Mary's appearances there in 1917, the great miracle of the sun event, and the predictions given by her to the children there, cannot be denied. The Church states you are not obliged to believe in the apparitions, but the accounts of what happened there can be found in the library of any major city. The rise of Communism, the start of World War

II, the destruction of Europe, persecution of the Church, all of these Fatima prophecies were fulfilled.

These events also led to one of the strongest periods of Marian devotion this country has ever seen. *The Legion of Mary*, detailed at the start of this book, sprang into existence, becoming one of the strongest parish organization and evangelizing tools in the Church. Rosary devotions became a standard, and the Family Rosary Crusade took to the airways. Father Peyton correctly admonished: "The family that prays together stays together." **The Blue Army** membership was now in the millions.

But it was all apparently supposed to take a nose-dive before embarking on this now current high. The 1960s and 70s came on the scene and brought with them the reasons for the fall as detailed earlier in this book.

And as also noted in the first two chapters of this book, Vatican II was not the only reason for the demise of the Church, or of the Marian Movement, or of the banishment of the Blessed Virgin. Individuals, as singular components of the Council, and acting under the so-called "spirit of Vatican II" (whatever that is), became culprits. The other components were probably social and moral decay, and those catch-all titles for rebellion: Secular Humanism, Modernism, Liberation Theology.

But prior to that fall of Marian devotions in the 60s and 70s, parish spirituality was a rather awesome sight. It carried over, obviously, into the schools and into the seminaries and convents. Does it really surprise anyone that family values and morals were shining stars at that time, and that drugs, violence, pornography, crime, and all of our current "contemporary advancements" were almost non-existent?

Various statistics available through the Church will also confirm that the great acceptance of Mary, and all of those devotions in use in her honor at that time were a shadow of the deep sense of commitment to the Church and the Sacraments. That would hardly seem a mere coincidence. It is more like living proof that Our Lady leads us to her Son, that where we honor and recognize her role in our lives, the gifts of the Holy Spirit are also that much more evident. In the past couple decades that has been most apparent through soaring private revelation and the regeneration of the Marian Movement and Charismatic Renewal.

And admittedly, there have been pitfalls to cope with in both movements. And why not. The forces of evil most certainly cannot just sit idly by, doing nothing, while watching more and more souls commit for God, declare Jesus as their Lord and Savior, and offer honor and devotion to His Mother. If the Marian Movement, just as the Charismatic Renewal found out, was not a most powerful force, Satan wouldn't waste his time with it, and there would be no problems in the private revelation arena. We will finish by speaking of some of that "power of the handmaid."

I believe Church history will verify that whenever the ordained Church seemed in particular peril or disarray, the faithful always came to the fore. The Holy Spirit has always touched the laity for that shot in the arm that may have been temporarily lacking for some reason on the part of the hierarchy. And it appears more often than not that the Blessed Virgin Mary was the instrument used by the Heavens to turn the people back to their Creator. The Virgin, at the urging of her Heavenly Spouse, comes to warn, to direct, to call her children back. Could it be otherwise if, in fact, she is the "Mother of the Church?"

Where Would We Be?

This book started with a question: "Where do you think the Church would be today without John Paul II, and without the Marian Movement?"

It is now time to answer that question. Never mind the apparitions and countless message books and predictions.

Where would the Church be without those two entities, John Paul II, and Marian devotion? It evokes some deep meditation.

The jury of the general populace is still out on this Slavic Pope, of course, just as it is on the current rage of Marian apparitions. Still, much can be said about him. Much cannot be denied about him. Personally, I believe history will regard him as one of the greatest person's to have lived in this century, and that the Church will one day recognize him as a saint. Regardless, there are certain givens, certain facts concerning this man that must be acknowledged.

He indeed is the world's ambassador, and no one can ever truthfully deny, or even question his contribution to mankind and his desire for peace. His love for people, regardless of race, gender, nationality, or even religious preference, is evident through his many pilgrimages into virtually every land on this planet. His prolific writings and homilies reflect a person of profound intellect and human understanding. Even his critics cannot deny that he is indeed a man of God.

Laurie Balbach-Taylor, in writing the Foreword for Michael Parker's book on the Pope, "*Priest of the World's Destiny*," provided a most excellent description of John Paul and his contributions. In part, she states:

"He is a student of the world and a teacher of its inhabitants. He is a devoted son of Poland and a citizen of the entire world. He is a faithful lamp of Jesus and a loyal shepherd to Jesus' flock. He is the pinpoint beam of light which directs our attention to the one true Light of the World, Jesus Christ. He is humble before God and humanity but intensely proud in his faith.

"As he draws crowds numbering in the millions with his charismatic personality, it is the substance of his speech which puts off his detractors. He is a threat. He understands and communicates, perhaps better than anyone else alive today, the interrelationships between people, communities, nations, and their God. He 'gets the big picture.' He exposes and manipulates the world's evils, in more dynamic and climactic ways than have ever been tried before—that they be destroyed. He is an appropriate conduit for the power of God.

"Those who love him love him intensely; they know his heart is with God. Those who oppose him fail to acknowledge the depth of Pope John Paul's perception and conviction. He has admirers and disparagers. But one thing is sure—no one can be indifferent to him."

Indeed, where would the Church be? He is an absolute light in the darkness . . . an ambassador of hope to all people of the world. He repeatedly upholds the teachings of the Church, to the point that it sometimes seems he stands alone against the world. It is evidenced by his position at

United Nations Conferences and other worldwide meetings of the powerful. He does not waiver in his faith, and especially in his zest for life. He accurately and courageously defines the "culture of death" as a hallmark of our era. He believes in his Church: in its teachings, it traditions, its founder. He has struggled to make sense out of decades of confusion and misinterpretation of Vatican II documents. He has affirmed Church teachings in profound encyclicals, whether popular themes or not, and has given us the "**New Catechism of the Catholic Church**." So strong is his pontificate that an attempt was made on his life.

His position as to the "Mother of the Church?" His pontificate is dedicated to her.

"**Totus Tuus**."

In 1987 he proclaimed only the second Marian Year in the history of the Church. Following the attempt on his life he traveled to the shrine of Fatima to thank "Our Lady of the Rosary" for sparing his life.

He in turn responded by consecrating the entire world to the Immaculate Heart of Mary.

He is a Polish Pope; a Marian Pope; a very Catholic Pope. He is a man of peace, of commitment, of courage. It is frightening to think of where the Church might be today had he not been here.

As to the role the Marian Movement plays in the Church, the Pope seems to have a very, very strong, if unofficial linking to this movement. In a January 3, 1996 address, he acknowledged the special role Mary played in the life of Christ and therefore, in salvation history. "Not only affection, but especially the light of the Spirit must lead us to understand the mother of Jesus and her contribution to the work of salvation," the Pope stated. He went on to add that though her role in salvation history is part of the mystery of Christian faith, Catholics must also **avoid** all attempts "to extend systematically to Mary the prerogatives of Christ and all the charisms of the Church."

As to addressing that question of where the church would be without the Marian devotions of the laity, we might first return once again for just a moment to the Holy Father. He is vitally aware of the importance of the Marian Movement and devotion to the Mother of God. In November of 1995, he gave an address on the importance of "Centers of Marian Piety." The Holy Father stated:

"The Church's Marian dimension is thus an undeniable element in the experience of the Christian people. It is not a superficial sentiment but a deep and conscious emotional bond, rooted in the faith which spurs Christians of the past and present to turn habitually to Mary, to enter into a more intimate communion with Christ . . .

"This message could not fail to be grasped by Christians called to a vocation of special consecration. In fact, Mary is particularly venerated in religious orders and congregations, and in institutes or associations of consecrated life. The spirituality of religious families, as well as of many ecclesial movements highlight their special bond with Mary as the guarantee of a charism fully and authentically lived. . . .

"This reverence to Mary binds not only committed Christians but also simple believers and even the 'distant,' for whom it is frequently their only link with the life of the Church. Pilgrimages to Marian shrines, which attract large crowds of the faithful throughout the year, are a sign of the Christian people's common sentiment for the Mother of the Lord. Some of these bulwarks of Marian piety are famous, such as Lourdes, Fatima, Loreto, Pompeii, Guadalupe and Czestochowa. Others are known only at the national or local level. In all of them, the memory of events associated with recourse to Mary conveys the message of her motherly tenderness, opening our hearts to God's grace. . . .

"These places of Marian prayer are a wonderful testimony to God's mercy, which reaches man through Mary's intercession. The miracles of physical healing, spiritual redemption, and conversion are the obvious signs that with Christ and in the Spirit, Mary is continuing her work as helper and mother. . . ."

But he also knows it is far more than just a superficial piety, or a pilgrimage to a shrine. It's based on the first official novena of the Church—Mary and the Holy Company in prayer awaiting the promised Holy Spirit. She was there then, she is here now.

Following the 1960s and 70s, the period of American social revolution and declining values, the Church found itself in similar doldrums. Spirituality was definitely on the decline—along with enrollment in seminaries and convents (nor could you find many that were even Catholic anymore). Sin was being re-defined and the birth control pill and the legalization of abortion were doing their part to help it along. Priests and nuns started bailing out and family values collapsed. Not surprisingly, education suffered and drugs and violence increased. Marian devotion had all but stopped.

But changing the Church norms regarding private revelation was only a partial cause of the re-birth of the Marian Movement. The major factor was simply that she was there, providing the renewal. She allegedly was there at Garabandal and then to a nun at Akita, Japan. She apparently was there for a priest named Stefano Gobbi and *"The Marian Movement of Priests"* began its international ministry. Then came claims from Betania, Venezuela, and Cuapa, Nicaragua. Behind the iron curtain the underground Church struggled under the leadership of Josyp Terelya, often imprisoned for his work. The renewal was formalized fifteen years ago in a tiny village called Medjugorje, in the former country of Yugoslavia. It was not just a broken Marian Movement she was renewing but a faltering Charismatic Renewal as well. The response of the faithful during this fifteen year period is probably the greatest spiritual movement the Church has seen in the past forty or fifty years.

Whether one cares to believe in Medjugorje or not is hardly the issue, but it is undeniable that Medjugorje was the fuse to the fireworks. Undeniable as well are the results.

In the 1980s the Rosary suddenly and dramatically returned to prominent use. Prayer groups, most of which were spawned at Medjugorje, started to spring up worldwide. The total became startling, quickly numbering in the thousands with hundreds of thousands of people participating. New Marian Centers came into existence and new apostolates and ministries sprang up across the land. In the United States alone, over 150 Marian organizations suddenly materialized, along with over five hundred major new prayer apostolates. New organizations involved in producing and distributing Marian materials became a major movement of its own in merely a ten year span. Conferences, workshops, seminars and Marian missions, all produced by the laity, the *"senus fidelium,"* became a continuous calendar of events across the country. Medjugorje became the conversion center of the entire world in only ten years. It became noted not for how many people claimed to have seen the Virgin Mary, but for how many Communions were distributed there, how many priests and pilgrims participated in the Mass there, and most important of all, how many people received the Sacrament of Reconciliation there. The number of Confessions heard at Medjugorje boggle the mind. Hundreds of bishops, thousands of priests have traveled to that tiny village. Their testimonies are legendary. The book, *In Testimony*, provides an excellent example, being the witnesses of over 80 priests and bishops on their experiences in Medjugorje. Paramount among those various experiences are the Confessions they heard there. It is mentioned continuously. The spiritual conversions and healings at Medjugorje stand head and shoulders above all other signs and wonders.

Almost 20,000,000 of the faithful have gone. Probably one percent might have experienced visions. Maybe twenty percent experienced some signs and wonders. Almost all experienced some spiritual benefit, some form of conversion, some special awareness. The results spread around the world. Marian devotion was back, and it is apparently the salvation of the Church. It is suddenly tens of millions strong.

You are vital!

Where would the Church be today without the Marian Movement? Just as with the case of not having John Paul II, the prospect is indeed frightening. I attempt here to answer that question by specifically addressing those involved in the Marian Movement, those currently devoting time and effort to Jesus Christ and His Church through the ministry and intercession of His Mother, and, I would also like to include myself in that number and as a part of that movement.

You, as the Marian Movement are the current foundation of the Church. You are the strength, the faith, the commitment. You are those who are out front, who wear their faith on their sleeve and are willing to proclaim it to all they meet.

It is you who have started all the prayer groups, who brought the Rosary back. It is you who are generally at daily Mass on a regular basis, who lead Rosary and litany devotions before or after.

It is you who are responsible for the initiation of countless peace Masses all over the country. It is you who have sponsored special Marian Masses and monthly programs. It is you who promote and call for a return to the Sacrament of Confession.

It is the Marian Movement who has been intricately involved with bringing Adoration of the Blessed Sacrament back to the Church. In a period when much of the spiritual elements and traditions of the Church have been cast aside, it is the Marian devotees who have been largely responsible for instigating Perpetual Adoration, or at least monthly or weekly Adoration in many parishes—parishes who then seem to flourish.

It is we in the Marian Movement who have provided major conferences and special Marian programs for all laity, and who have used modern communications to bring Mary to millions of people in one form or another.

It is we who are involved in the prayer cenacles, who offer daily and weekly intercession for the needs of so many. It is we who are constantly praying for the ordained Church, for bishops, priests, nuns and brothers, and for more and stronger vocations.

It is usually Marian devotees who are active in intercession for the halt of abortion, or who are present in prayer before abortion clinics. We are active in kindergarten, CCD, youth groups, retreats, and RCIA. We are the promoter of "Divine Mercy Cenacles" and "Marian Movement of Priest Cenacles."

We who are involved in the Marian Movement are the backbone of consecration efforts to the Sacred Heart of Jesus and the Immaculate Heart of Mary.

You are the strongest spiritual force in the Church today. How many are aware that over 10,000 special, additional Masses have been added throughout the world, per year, because of the efforts of the Marian Movement? Are you aware that worldwide these new groups pray approximately 5,000,000 Rosaries every day—and which means 250,000,000 Hail Mary's are offered daily to the Heavens in intercession?

Along with Medjugorje becoming the reconciliation and conversion center of the world, apparition sites and shrines have brought untold thousands back to the Church and the Sacraments, while other parish efforts to do so often achieve little or no results. Speakers, books and videos have additionally led a great number back to the faith. Fortunately, no one has to just accept my word for it. The Riehle Foundation has received many thousands of letters and testimonials from people from all walks of life who attest to being especially touched or led by something they have read or seen. Dozens of other ministries can and do stress the same.

All of this has been realized in just the past fifteen years.

You—the Marian Movement—you are the Church. You are the Renewal. You are the prayer groups, the Rosaries, the Masses, the intercession. You are the spiritual center of the Catholic faith. You are the foundation of the Church.

You are the wall—the last wall—between the Mystical Body of Christ and Satan. You are the most vital link for the preservation of the Church. You are at the forefront, and do not doubt for an instant that Pope John Paul II and the Holy See are not totally aware of it. It is necessary to guard and preserve this great gift.

That is why it is so important that all in the Marian Movement become aware of the pitfalls in private revelation. That is why we cannot let the Marian Movement come apart or let Satan and the forces of evil further delude or deceive. Consider for a moment here, once again, where the Church would be today without the above identified effort.

If someone can identify a stronger spiritual organization or entity in the Catholic Church today, I would appreciate hearing from them with the details of such an organization or movement.

Lines for the Sacrament of Reconciliation are always obvious at apparition sites and special Marian Masses and conferences. How long are the confession lines at the average American parish? Can you even find parishes that promote confessions?

There is no lack of enthusiasm or effort, and no dissatisfaction with Masses, prayers and singing at those same Marian Masses and liturgies. Can the average American parish say as much today for its Sunday crowd?

How many people, in any parish, actively involved in prayer groups, weekday Mass, Adoration of the Blessed Sacrament, Right to Life, Rosary or Divine Mercy Cenacles, Bible study groups, Parent/teacher organizations, etc. are not also active in Marian Devotion?

Can any parish pastor accurately define the "spiritual strength" of his parishioners as coming from: Peace and social justice issues, discussion groups, bingo and social functions, the parish picnic, men's and women's social/civic groups within the parish, or any one of a dozen other committees or organizations active within the parish? Are they all worthwhile, and do they have merit? Of course. But do they constitute the spiritual foundation of the parish? Is the Church faced with any empty convents and seminaries, disgruntled once a week Catholics, empty confessionals, apathy, dissension within the ranks, open rebellion as to Church doctrines, and Catholic schools which no longer are? And if the Episcopate feels it is sinking in the quicksand of "pro-choice," "gay rights," the ordination of women or married clergy, sexual scandal in the Church, and theologians who pull more and more people away from Catholic teaching, where do the bishops find good, solid spiritual support for their needs? Where do they find the prayer warriors, the intercessors? From the CHD coffers? From peace and social justice advocates, or from any of the above referenced dissent groups?

Who do you really think is most involved in praying for the Church, for her bishops and priests, brothers and nuns? An affiliation of theologians and college professors?

Or is it the people actively involved in the Marian Movement?

Can you begin to comprehend the size and scope of this

movement? The numbers involved and the spiritual power it possesses? Can you see why it is so necessary for Satan to try to destroy it? In just the United States alone, in the past ten years, can you imagine how many tens of thousands of pilgrims struggled all the way to former Yugoslavia and back—not to mention additional tens of thousands that traveled to American shrines and claimed apparition sites? Can you envision the depth of the faith commitment being offered as witness?

More importantly, from the 172 Marian Organizations and Centers in this country, the total number of Marian Movement of Priest Cenacles, the Marian conferences, retreats and special monthly or weekly Masses, can you imagine how many people are being reached? How many parishes have returned to the recognition and importance of Adoration of the Blessed Sacrament at a time when so many are completely indifferent to the Real Presence?

Would anyone (read "bishops") care to poll the number of Catholics who have **returned** to the Church and the Sacraments in the past ten years and ask them just what brought them back? What do you think they are going to say? Was it bingo? The Church's position on immigration?

Marian devotion (and that term has spread today to definitely include **devotion to the Sacred Heart of Jesus and the Immaculate Heart of Mary**), is the last line of defense in the spiritual warfare currently raging in the world in general, and in the Church in particular. There are those who see Marian devotees as "apparition chasers." And indeed there are some of those. But by and large we are pretty solid people with our heads screwed on straight. Often it seems our spiritual commitment is higher than what we find available in our parishes. At times, it may even be hardly existent in our parishes. So some go where the action is—where spirituality is promoted, not snubbed.

What if the bishops in the United States literally harnessed all of this energy and used it in concert with the needs of the Church? What if they brought it all back into the Church in a united effort? What if it functioned just like the Legion of Mary functioned—as an integral part of parish devotion? Wow! Wouldn't that be something! What a force!

Dioceses that stress Perpetual Adoration, the Marian Movement, The Right to Life, the Sacraments, seem to prosper. Why? Peoria, San Antonio, and New Orleans, are just a few examples. It is hardly a coincidence. Why does Peoria draw strong Catholic candidates to its seminaries? What a tremendous, powerful, prayer army is available to the Church in the form of Marian devotion. All it has to do is be utilized.

Satan knows that. He also believes in God. He also knows of the Blessed Virgin Mary. As previously stated, he is familiar with all of our devotions and is totally aware of what is being said at every claimed apparition site in the world. He knows false apparitions encourage the sensational, their emphasis on multiplying prayers and devotions causing pressure and scrupulosity and guilt feelings. He knows some temporary good fruits might turn out to be total abandonment of what could have been a good thing.

He knows the strength of Marian Devotion, that it has long been a key element to the prosperity and continuation of the Church. What an enormous victory if he could somehow actually use that very movement to destroy itself, and hopefully, the Church in general along with it! According to several doctors and early fathers of the Church, that has exactly been his plan. If so, it seems he is going full steam ahead with it today.

There are twenty five years of evidence to support all of that, in that the Catholic Charismatic Renewal is a most interesting parallel.

To some the Charismatic Renewal, and its counterpart in Evangelical and Pentecostal denominations, was the work of Satan. Actually, I think his work was only in trying to destroy it all. At any rate, the Charismatic phenomena was an accurate forerunner of the private revelation craze of today. Fr. Michael Scanlon was quoted earlier in this book in making some interesting comparisons between the two. It was noted that too often in the renewal movement, certain charisms claimed by participants would run sort of out of control (and we sure have a bunch of visionaries today who fall under that same diagnosis). Too often the movement seemed to be fighting the Church (or vice versa) instead of trying to become an integral part of it. The ordained Church on its part was just as guilty. There was great spirituality in the movement, tremendous energy, many gifts and charisms, and all of that simply adds up to enormous strength in the areas of evangelization and conversion. Millions of people responded. So strong was the spirituality of the movement that those not prone to open and enthusiastic displays of faith (laity and clergy alike) looked upon it as evil. The evil was that Satan, as with the current Marian Movement, knew he had to infiltrate it, divide it, confuse it, and mislead it.

That becomes much easier to do when the Church is not actively supporting it, or providing leadership or guidance—another parallel we see with the Marian Movement today. The result was that the Charismatic Renewal became fractionalized, and many of its membership fell away. Much of the impetus was lost. Satan was probably elated.

The positive news today is that there are some very strong connections developing between the Marian and Charismatic Movements, and they are in position to be harnessed by the Church. What if the bishops, as suggested above, added one million additional members of the Charismatic Renewal to this great Marian energy they wished to harness for the benefit of the Church? How much more power would then be added? What a prayer force! What a threat to the prince of this world in his efforts to destroy the Church! The time is ripe to put it all together. Is that the "unity" Our Lord speaks of?

As noted, the Marian Movement may be the final wall between the Mystical Body of Christ and Satan. You are that important to the Church. We must not let the forces of evil deceive us in our efforts for the honor and glory of God, through the ministry of "the Handmaid of the Lord."

The Power of the Handmaid

Given the fact that there is such a contrast and difference of opinion pertaining to private revelation and the role of Mary in our salvation journey, it may be worth taking a few additional pages to summarize the apparent power given to the Madonna by the Almighty. As she has stated in her **Magnificat**: *"Henceforth all generations shall call me blessed; Because He who is mighty has done great things for me . . ."*

Besides, don't you think it's really a little too late to start doubting the power of the Almighty? That also goes for the power of "the Handmaid of the Lord" as well. She has always been there. In our own century, at the incredible events at Fatima, she was the focal point. And her prophecies rang true.

Perhaps those who have some doubts as to her presence, or her power, might want to count the number of wheelchairs and crutches at Lourdes.

Ultimately, it may not be that important as to whether that power and presence is attributed to Mary, or to the Lord. What is important is that we recognize that it exists—just as we need to recognize that God exists. And that awesome power can and does act as to the needs of mankind whether we are properly attuned, or whether we aren't. As mentioned previously, great signs and wonders happened at Bayside, New York, and at Necedah, Wisconsin. They still do. And at other apparitions sites as well that have not been approved by the Church.

There is a common, and well founded statement: "God can and does produce good out of bad." I believe that. And why shouldn't He recognize the efforts, faith and belief of thousands of people who gather at such and such a site for His honor and glory—regardless of whether a claimed visionary is authentic or not. And indeed He has responded. To those who experienced a physical healing—perhaps more importantly, a spiritual one—no confirmation of a visionary's authenticity is necessary. To those who have witnessed the supernatural manifestations of God, who have experienced the outpouring of grace, who have been touched by Mary in a personal way, there is no need to try to explain that power.

The peace the **Lady** brings is a hallmark of her appearances. It matches the peace Her Son always brought with Him and so often spoke about. That peace is a great "evaluator" in the discernment of apparitions, and it is very lacking in so many of them today where the messages are all chastisement, and threats, and confusion and power struggles. All of that comes from the wrong spirit and "sells" sensationalism.

It becomes very difficult to understand how peace can replace power and strength sometimes. Just like "turning the other cheek" often causes us to wince. Then on top of that, we are expected to accept that she always just picks plain ol' people instead of appearing to Cardinals and Popes—or even presidents. Why is that?

Maybe she got it from Her Son. Look at some of the people He picked. Saul, Judas, Mary Magdalene? A group of uneducated fisherman? Let's face it; if she can pick me for some role in her army, she could pick anybody—and probably has. And as we struggle, as we mess up a lot of it along the way, as we get the wrong spirits intermingled in it all, as our ego and pride seem to take over, or at least interfere, the Blessed Virgin Mary, through the Grace of the Almighty Who has done great things for her, continues to do great things for us. It has happened at many current claimed apparition sites, including Conyers, Georgia, for example, where there is probably reason to question the whole thing, but where signs and wonders still occur; or Cold Springs, Kentucky, or Santa Maria, California, or Marlboro, New Jersey. Wherever spiritual warfare is in full array, wherever the forces of good and evil are locked in open combat, look for the power of the Heavens to manifest itself in some way, and in spite of our downfallen human nature. The only problem then, that eternal one, the one we have been trying to identify for many pages here, is one of discernment. That means beware of the fact that the wrong spirit can produce some pretty spectacular displays of his own.

The number of miracles, especially in the form of physical and spiritual healings, attributed to the Blessed Virgin Mary at apparition sites the world over is indeed mind boggling. Literally millions and millions can attest to it. Such are all those abandoned crutches at Lourdes. Such are all those tearful confessions and return to the Sacraments at Fatima and other sites. Such is the return to the Blessed Sacrament, the tremendous rise in new prayer groups and the return to the Rosary today. Her power, though, is not simply manifested at apparition sites and shrines. She produces good fruits through her chosen children and through those called to witness in all facets of everyday life.

And most certainly, there has been and currently is more good than questionable involved in those who work in her ministry and for the honor and glory of Her Son today. We need to recognize that very many people have apparently perceived a certain call, and have responded, and by their own admission experienced a certain outpouring of grace to the benefit of their souls. They have accepted that grace, without seeking fame, publicity, or economic gain. They are the people who comprise that army of devotees noted in the previous ten pages.

Because of the current vast network of Marian devotion in this country, we can identify many of those efforts, individually and collectively. It includes tens of thousands who have responded nationally to numerous days of prayer or special liturgies, regardless of inconveniences such as weather. It includes the hundreds of thousands who have heard Bud Macfarlane speak or listened to his excellent tapes on apparitions. It includes taking the image of Our Lady of Guadalupe literally into the streets, especially at abortion clinics and putting prayer cards, rosaries, new devotionals and hymns into the hands of millions of people nationally.

Michael Brown has reached hundreds of thousands through his books, such as *The Final Hour*, and through countless speaking engagements. He like many others has been a highly effective and sought after personality for radio talk shows and TV programs. Our Lady has called many and captured many hearts along the way. Her army is strongly entrenched, though under severe attack, and has utilized mass communications to go along with the signs and wonders phenomena attracting so many millions. EWTN television has been joined by national network television in reporting the presence of the supernatural, albeit the national networks sometimes get the wrong spirits lumped in, in the process. Regardless, many, many millions of hearts and souls have been touched in the past fifteen years.

It includes a number of Marian organizations who send out various newletters, newspapers and magazines. In our case, *The Blue Letter* newsletter reaches in excess of 25,000 people every month. The touch of "the Handmaid of the Lord" is indeed vast, and powerful. While the world struggles in its "culture of death," while the Church copes with division and confusion, the Mother of the Savior comes to tell her children, *"do whatever He tells you."*

It includes thousands of priests and bishops who are members of Marian Apostolates, such as *The Marian Move-*

ment of Priests, and who serve as spiritual directors and confessors for numerous other apostolates. Most importantly, it is this body of involved priests and bishops who can best attest as to how many souls have been touched, how many conversions have occurred, how many have returned to the Sacraments. That is why it is so necessary to define some situations that can drain its strength and credibility. It is not just a claimed visionary or apparition site that we are questioning; it may be the work of that evil spirit, long recognized for deceiving us with false messages of light. He was there at the start of the Bible, in *Genesis*, Chapter 3. And he is still there in the last book of the Bible, *Revelations*, where Satan tries to snatch the new-born child away from the Woman Clothed with the Sun (Chapter 12).

Let us state again, you are vital to the Church and perhaps a last line of spiritual strength in a world that desperately needs some spiritual strength. You are aligned with "The Mother of the Church." We must guard and protect this movement at any cost, at any price, for the enemy of the Lord is committed to try and destroy it. Along the way, all of us as active members of the Marian Movement, are probably going to have to come to grips with the possibility that we might also be deceived in the realm of private revelation. Maybe deliberately so; maybe not intentionally.

Please recognize and accept the reality of this spiritual warfare. We see that same confusion in other aspects of the Church, in vocations, in the difficulties present in families today. But the good is still the stronger. Satan still faces two major roadblocks—Her army, and Her Pope.

And as to the power of evil? False apparitions or messages? The occult? New Age counterfeits?

Jesus Christ is infinitely stronger. He is a bigger Savior than we are sinners. He is a bigger Savior than all of those false movements put together. All we have to do is our part.

CHAPTER 6

Defining the Problem and Solution

It's pretty evident that spiritual warfare is in full bloom. It's seen in all aspects of our world. It is also pretty evident that the forces of evil are attacking the Marian Movement just as they have targeted the priesthood and the family.

There is also a need to recognize that God does not abandon His people. He does not leave us orphans. In this era of profound spiritual warfare, He most certainly provides Heavenly assistance to us. His graces are there, if only we are open to them. Traditionally, a lot of this assistance to us has come from His Mother. There is really far too much such activity today to continue to doubt that is exactly what is happening.

The guy on the other side of the spiritual warfare line of combat doesn't doubt it. As such, he needs to seriously try to destroy her visitations (and those of her Son), or at least infiltrate them. Thus we have the need here to attempt to zero in on the specific problems in private revelation.

Perhaps we can pare it down to three specific areas: The laity, the bishops and priests, and third, the Marian promoters.

162

The Laity

Our own in-house, informal survey shows that many people become involved with private revelation because they are spiritually starved. They simply state that they are not being fed spiritually from the pulpit and that they seldom hear anymore any of the traditional beliefs associated with the Catholic Church. Included is Marian devotion (not to mention, sin, the Sacrament of Confession, the True Presence, Hell, Purgatory, etc.). As a result, they gravitate toward those issues or places that are more steeped in spiritual elements, that appear more closely connected to the supernatural (or at least appear so).

The obvious response to that, I suppose, would be: "How can you get more connected than through the Eucharist and the Mass?"

And, I guess the obvious answer to that would be: "You can't—if in fact you're getting a full dose of just how awesome it is at the Mass you are attending in your parish setting." The complaint is that often that Mass is very un-fulfilling.

There have also been those who have tried to promote the idea that people tend to chase after any claimed visionary when they become overwhelmed by the faults of society, or frightened by claimed conditions in the world or the Church.

Frankly, that seems like a rather poor cop-out. I am sure that a certain percentage of people involved in pursuits of private revelation do fit that mold. But, by and large, most of these people are very devout, totally committed to the Church, and to the Blessed Virgin Mary, dedicated to the Magisterium, and at times a step above most of their fellow parishioners in their faith and commitment.

That seems to be the situation for most of us at the start. However, it also seems that many of us are in the process of losing some of those traits as the crescendo of claimed apparitions and signs and wonders continue. Caught up in the sensationalism of more and more projected revelation and prophecy, the discerning eye can give way to emotions and false hope. At that point anything is possible.

The faithful are not subject to any controls and oftentimes have no Church authorized leadership, or guidelines. Without it, they can find themselves faced with the possibility that they are disobeying the Blessed Virgin Mary, or her Son, by opposing some seer or message that seems totally right and in accordance with Church teaching. Discernment is then completely abandoned, and admittedly, in some cases it was never even started to begin with. Chastisement, the big item today, is the hallmark of sensationalism, and there is plenty of sensationalism to go around. Signs and wonders abound. We are right back to spiritual entertainment.

The final result is that sooner or later we might reach the point where nothing is being discerned; everything and everyone is believed; you-know-who becomes involved in much of it; no direction is provided; and a whole bunch of very devout and committed people (including clergy) are deceived—I guess just exactly the way the Bible told us they would. There is an urgent and immediate need for all of us to simply question more of these messages and prophecies, take nothing for granted, and be very cautious in the field of private revelation. It is a need to return to the basics of our faith.

The Ordained Church

Many bishops do not get involved. It is that simple. It is very disconcerting. It is sad. There are many theories: They don't care. They are opposed to Mary. They don't believe in apparitions. They are too caught up in peace and social justice issues, or inclusive language, or rewriting the Bible, or on and on and on. Perhaps all of the above is correct. Perhaps none of it. But in all probability, a little is, most isn't.

Regardless, there is a need first of all to recognize and accept the position of the Church with respect to private revelation. We have referred to it repeatedly in this book. The Church has been dealing with supernatural phenomena since its inception and is very cautious in its discernment process (as we should be). Recognizing this, and knowing that private revelation can add nothing to the faith as revealed by God, it doesn't make a whole lot of sense for any bishop to get too excited at the outset over any claimed apparition. It appears the same scenario is present at the parish level and with the parish pastor.

On the other hand, there are some pretty important "givens" here.

1) There are too many claimed heavenly manifestations for at least some of them not to be true.
2) There are some pretty heavy duty miracles involved in much of this that cannot be disproven.
3) The people involved in the Marian Movement, and the *"senus fidelium"* present, is not the result of a group of crackpots having too much of the bubbly.
4) While the Church has ruled against a number of these claimed private revelations, a number of others have been approved, and many others are now being seriously investigated.
5) There are some positive fruits and benefits available to the Church here, if proper direction is given.

The key seems to be "proper direction" (as opposed to no direction at all, perhaps). As we've noted throughout this book, there has been a certain "loosening" of restrictions concerning private revelation and much more freedom for the faithful as well. Then too, while the documents of Vatican II and the new Catechism allude to the reality and the acceptance of private revelation, the fact of the matter is that the ordained Church has been very slow to pursue the graces and gifts these charisms can provide, if proven authentic.

Complete disregard by the bishops and priests would mean some claimed apparitions that had real value were lost. And others, infiltrated by the wrong spirit, or taken over by the human spirit because of lack of direction, should have been eliminated early on and were not.

In recent months, the Church has moved against a number of alleged seers and apparition sites. Personally, I am pleased to see some action taken, even if it is negative. However, in most cases, it is late in coming.

If there is no direction, no guidance, no involvement by the bishop, who bears the responsibility for these occurrences in his diocese? If the ordained Church is not willing to become involved, and the events erode, then sooner or later the bishop will be called in, and at that point, he will probably come in with hatchet in hand to put a stop to something that has gone out of control. That is sad, and, totally worthless to all elements of the Church.

In some cases, a local bishop has been openly condemning of the events, before the fact (Medjugorje); in other cases, he took no position whatsoever or refused to recognize anything (Cincinnati/Kentucky). To be sure, some have probably been approved prematurely, and others were left to simply be lost in a sea of confusion, doubt, skepticism and rebuke, without ever having a chance. Some bishops also need to be applauded for their concern, their interest and involvement, and for their willingness to make a decision accordingly (Denver, Colorado).

One thing is certain. These manifestations are **not** going to go away. Not after being part of our faith since the beginning of time. And in a world that is on the threshold of destroying itself, the teaching authority of the Catholic Church, being the conference of bishops for a given country or region of the world, truly needs to get involved with our Creator's efforts to personally reach His people. The Conference of Bishops in this country needs to avail itself of the fervor and commitment of the laity involved in the Marian Movement, (and the Charismatic Renewal), and further, provide some specific guidelines to follow in the area of discernment, not only for the Marian devotees, but for those engaged in the business aspects of producing the materials that are being swallowed up all over the country and the world today.

It is hard to believe that it is in the best interest of the Church for the bishops and priests to sit idly by, uninvolved, while dozens of self-proclaimed prophets, would-be theologians and doctors of mystical theology, or claimed experts on the projected end times, provide the faithful with all kinds of information and materials that can have but limited value for the salvation of their souls—but maybe many more negative implications.

Obviously, the answer is not for the ordained Church to take the position of: "OK, we'll just abolish all of it." That has been tried in one way or another forever. Besides, as Gamaliel accurately told the Sanhedrin: *"If this comes from God, you will not be able to destroy them; you may even find yourselves fighting against God"* (*Acts* 5:39). But it would seem that a statement of involvement, or cooperation and/or support from the Bishops, collectively, could go a long, long way toward stabilizing this very touchy spiritual issue which is flying largely out of control today.

Promoters and Professionals

That means people like me—those of us who are involved in some professional capacity in the Marian Movement. And, we might be the biggest problem of all. The amount of material available today, dealing with various aspects of mystical theology, visions, apparitions, supernatural manifestations of one form or another, is truly staggering. And most of it involves the Blessed Virgin Mary. In second place is the angel interest, and New Age devotees are involved in both.

I guess we could define this "professional" aspect as all those involved in writing, publishing, producing, promoting, and marketing Marian materials or materials dealing with private revelation, as well as those who are involved in the fringe areas but who are not commercially oriented. They would be represented by many Marian apostolates and centers, and for the most part, they are often non-profit in their goals and structures.

But the commercial side of the private revelation business is growing by leaps and bounds and unfortunately, we seem to be loosing our scruples along the way. Mary and apparitions have become a business. A very, very, big business. In the past five years, probably a $100 million dollar business in this country.

Once again, a major part of the overall problem seems to be Church authorized. It comes from the elimination of Canons #1399 and #2318 of the former *Code of Canon Law* by Pope Paul VI. It simply means that no "Imprimatur" is required for material dealing with private revelation. In videos, at the start of the film, you will often see the following statement. In books, it appears on the copyright page:

In conformity with the decrees of Pope Urban VIII, the Publisher recognizes and accepts that the final authority regarding these messages rests with the Holy See of Rome, to whose judgment we willingly submit.

The decree of the Congregation for the Propagation of the Faith A.A.S. 58, 1186 (approved by Pope Paul VI on October 14, 1966) states that the *Imprimatur* is no longer required on publications that deal with new revelations, apparitions, prophesies or miracles, provided that they contain nothing contrary to faith and morals.

The elimination of the above restrictions concerning the publishing of books was widely hailed as a great step forward for the Church. And I guess it was. It certainly opened the flood gates for private revelation. At the same time, as previously stated, the Church re-structured its guidelines on the judging of private revelations (the Cardinal Seper Document of 1978), along with acknowledging a general freedom of opinion in the use of the printed word.

Though the positive results of those moves probably cannot be questioned, it has now reached the point where some further action probably needs to be taken. There is one line in the above publisher's statement that is of prime importance. It states: "Provided that they contain nothing contrary to faith and morals." Or nothing that is opposed to the established doctrine of the Church.

I wonder if anyone of Church authority checked all of the books published in the past ten years dealing with private revelations to determine if there was anything there that was questionable. You can bet not. Further, very few were even submitted for review. I know, for I plead guilty as well.

This means that anyone: any publisher, organization, individual, anyone who claims he or she is a visionary, or any one who wishes to be one, can publish a book without Church approval by simply sticking a certain statement on the copyright page of a book.

Any publisher who wishes to promote some view of mystical theology, end times, chastisement, or promote any specific claimed seer or some view of private revelation, need only state that the book deals with private revelation and stick the proper paragraph on the copyright page. Anyone who wishes to become an expert in the interpretation of Scripture, or the "why's and how's" of the coming chastisement, or who thinks he or she can explain God's ultimate plan for the world need only label such views as "private revelation" and stick the statement on the copyright page. False mystics and New Age proponents have thus had easy access.

As noted previously, in compiling this book, I had the opportunity to research—or in many cases browse through—a truly, huge stack of books dealing with private revelations. All were published in the past fifteen years. It was two stacks each, and three feet high. She has become big business. Money then becomes a motivator as well.

Are those of us in the communications industry now doing our part to add to the confusion? Are we inviting the wrong spirits into this vast maze of supernatural intervention by our willingness to print anything and everything, often without question?

Between the laity, as a growing army of devotees, and the professional industry, as the production and communication link throughout the world, have we reached the point where we believe the entire Marian Movement is indestructible . . . that this ship is too big to go down . . . that like the *Titanic*, it is unsinkable?

Well, water is coming in! Is anybody paying attention?

"How many is too much?" In the appendix of this book there is a list shown under that title. It is a summary list of visionaries and apparition sites. It doesn't rate them, or approve or disapprove, or attempt to authenticate or condemn. It's just simply a list. The really scary part is that it's only a partial list.

The Positives: A Solution?

Still, the **really good news** is that the positives seem to far outweigh the negatives.

Let's start with my profession, since it definitely appears to be the biggest problem at this point. It is also an emerging force that can produce a positive spiritual renewal that is beyond calculation.

In 1986, Fran (my deceased wife) and I went on a pilgrimage to Europe—principally to Fatima and Medjugorje. It was a trip of commitment, of consecration. And for many others on that trip, it was also the fruition of a searching. The number of ministries, apostolates, businesses and Marian centers that resulted from that trip is truly amazing. It became evident to most of us that we were somehow called.

Included on that pilgrimage were Terry Colafrancesco, who then built the organization, **Caritas of Birmingham**; Fran and Bill Reck and the emergence of **The Riehle Foundation** and **Faith Publishing Company** on an international basis; Rosalie Turton who now heads up the **101 Foundation**; and the spiritual director of the pilgrimage, a priest by the name of **Fr. Ken Roberts**, whose Marian ministry was to take him to worldwide prominence. In addition to these people, whose activity was to take on a more professional role, the pilgrimage roster included a whole line-up of people who founded prayer groups, peace centers, Medjugorje centers, and local or parish organizations that blossomed into strong spiritual renewal movements.

That story was to be repeated in similar situations many times over the next half-a-dozen years, in many other parts of the world. Mary was openly recruiting for the build-up of her army. She was calling many, and from all walks of life. Lives and careers were changed in a heartbeat. Your life now became a commitment to her ministry, and for the honor and glory of her Son. Hundreds of others followed suit, traveled the same pilgrimage route, and found the same result. It was person by person, ministry by ministry, city by city, region by region, seer by seer, and priest by priest.

Interestingly, through all of that in the past fifteen years, it was not the large, established, professional organizations in the communication/publishing industry that responded (read "picked") to this re-birth of Marian devotion. New ministries and new careers were forged—and with incredible success. Many were based on a "non-profit" structure, as was the case with so many Marian centers that sprang up across the country and around the world. Their activities and efforts were obviously resoundly blessed. The fruits were very positive, easily discernible, and undeniable. They were built around a return to the Sacraments, to prayer, and to the Church, not just a vision or some sign or wonder.

This new force of professional activity in the Marian Movement may have produced more material dealing with the Blessed Virgin Mary than the Church had seen in a hundred years. It reached more people, and brought more people back into the mainstream of the faith than anything the hierachical Church had done. The efforts touched souls, reached hearts, and put meaning into struggling lives and spiritual emptiness.

But eager souls and hearts aren't always alert to issues of discernment. They are much more open to claimed words from Jesus or His Mother. And those eager souls responded.

And who can say it has not produced phenomenal results?

There appears to be only one problem. It seems to now be flying out of control, with no pilot.

Perhaps we could all meditate a little on this following scenario. First of all, there is a pilot. He is called the Pope. There is leadership through the teaching authority of the Church, its Magisterium, and this includes the College of Bishops. We already have enough claimed experts in doctrine and Scripture (probably too many), and they are known as theologians. Maybe all we need to do is to simply accept it all, to recognize that this authority exists, and utilize it.

If that be so, perhaps then the only other need is to discern and control the day to day activity in the private revelation realm by combining the assistance of bishops and priests, those of the faithful involved in the movement, and the efforts of those of us who are involved in the production of materials and information.

The Church needs to take an active position in the hotbed of private revelation. Sloughing it off or putting it down is self-defeating and seemingly will result in the loss of great graces, as well as causing untold future pain. No one in the ordained Church can accurately say that God is not currently speaking to His people. On the other hand, some of these claimed mystical experiences are obviously not in the best interest of the faith and truly need to be curtailed.

The power, the force, the commitment, the spirituality available to the Church through those involved in the Marian Movement is enormous. Is the Church so strong today, so at peace, so much in agreement, so successful in its agendas, that She can afford to look the other way? Do the bishops really believe that the strength of the Church, its future and its success is going to be predicated on inclusive language, or reworking the liturgy? Do the bishops really believe that peace and social justice issues, stomping for married clergy or gay rights is more vital to the current condition of the Church than is prayer? Or the Eucharist and Perpetual Adoration? Dear bishops; could you use about one million profound prayer warriors in America to intercede every day for the Church and your needs? All they need is a little recognition—and direction.

The Laity, it seems, aside from desperately needing some guidance and direction from the Church, also needs to adhere to accepted standards of discernment. This current craze of complete acceptance of a visionary and his/her messages because one is afraid of opposing the Blessed Virgin Mary is really a little absurd. It is repeatedly stated that no one is obliged to believe in any private revelation, but today, it seems that for many, it is more credible than the *New Catechism*, or even the *Bible*.

No visionary is going to save your soul by virtue of just some message or prophecy, and no claimed expert in mystical theology can add one single thing about the chastisement or the end times to the deposit of faith.

The history of the Church has repeatedly shown that the trust and faith of the people is a cornerstone of the Church; and it is further a great strength in the discernment of all private revelation. But it takes participation on our part. It seems, perhaps, like a technological world, so advanced in its methods and instruments of mass communication, has taken away this sense of a need for evaluation. It is something we urgently need to recapture. The Holy Spirit still speaks to us through our hearts, our minds, and so does our Lord, His Mother, and our guardian angels. We need to listen. If anything in the area of private revelation brings any doubt to your mind, any confusion, any uneasiness, any conflict or doubt, drop it. You don't need it, and it is probably not from God to begin with.

My profession, the **Publishing/Communication** component of the Marian Movement has done a truly remarkable and amazing job of reaching people worldwide in the past

15 years on behalf of the Marian Movement (in spite of me, perhaps). The new ministries and apostolates formed to serve those involved in Marian devotion, and by its very nature the Sacred Heart of Jesus, the Sacraments, and the Church in general, literally became a whole new and vital conduit of Catholic communication. It provided the impetus for this great surge of Marian spirituality, untold conversions, and currents of prayer. It also provided the impetus for increased private revelation.

The commitment and zeal of those in this industry may be unmatched in any other facet of Catholic communications. Not only have they taken on the responsibility of producing and distributing new materials, they have also been key players in all other forms of communications.

What we haven't done is apply the brakes when needed, discerned our efforts and motives as required, or stepped up to the plate to take a responsible position of leadership in the ever present need for discernment. Whether any other faction or entity stepped into the breach to lead in the area of discernment is not the issue. Our audience, or market as it were, is enormous and no one can reach it faster and easier than we can. This has now taken on additional, frightening implications as we confront the rush to evangelize through the use of the computer and the internet—a freedom to promote all kinds of movements.

Those involved in producing material dealing with private revelation probably need to police themselves. It does not appear anyone else is going to do it, and the interest of the Magisterium of the Church in providing a certain freedom for the publication of materials through the elimination of a need for "*imprimaturs*" is hardly a justification for simply adding a certain statement to the copyright of a book, and publishing anything that comes along. The responsibility we have for the direction people might take because of the influence of materials we have provided them is great indeed.

That responsibility might also include a certain amount of integrity as to economic gain. We all need to address that issue ourselves, individually, but there is little doubt that the business end of private revelation should be a very key part of the evaluation process of the Church in judging apparitions. If it were the only ingredient judged today, many, if not most apparitions and the visionaries involved, would be disqualified.

Neither Mary nor her Son is requesting us to publish more books or videos. That is simply our doing. Nor are they asking us to produce $3,000 statues, $250 gold or silver plated medals, $50 rosaries or a whole raft of items from coffee cups to T-shirts. They just keep telling us the need is to pray, to fast, to convert, to come back to the Sacraments. They keep telling us about the "Divine Mercy," not how we are going to get zapped with a fireball.

The Marian Movement has a tremendous contingent of writers, speakers, producers, publishers, and various organizations and apostolates at its disposal. And it is worldwide in scope, and overall, principally endorsed by the Magisterium of the Church. But we need to police our activities and establish guidelines where they are needed, like how the chastisement is going to come down, or when, or where. We need to accept the fact that we don't really know that, and neither does any visionary. We need to back off from the fantasy of becoming an instant theologian. Church Doctrine is in the hands of the Magisterium of the Church—where it has always been, and should be.

Maybe the most important thing we need to do is to attempt to link up this profession with the ordained Church and with all of us who compromise the lay-faithful in the Marian Movement . . . combine forces, talents, efforts. I wonder if that's the unity we really need. I wonder if some of us spin wheels endlessly in an effort to unite all religions and churches in some false idea of ecumenism, and here Jesus and His Mother are merely telling us: "Get your own act together first."

I guess first of all, that means my own. This book probably didn't require Church approval, but I've published some others that could have benefitted from it. At least, we should consider some form of Church endorsement or recognition. Recognition or acceptance by a priest or bishop, as to basic content, is something this ministry will consider essential to future publishing as far as private revelation is concerned.

The Supreme Being changes all in a split second. He simply points a finger and an empire lays in ruins. He simply wills it and an unexplainable healing instantly occurs. His Mother comes to tell us to "simplify our lives," and we take that to mean we are somehow to add to our importance and cleverness. It can be gone in an instant.

And if a chastisement comes, of what use is all of our ministries and our cleverness? Of what value is all of our computers, and fax machines and telephones, and copiers? All of a sudden your "web page" is worthless because the internet no long functions—nor does your fax machine.

We also must police ourselves. Money cannot continue to be a root cause for pumping out all kinds of new sensationalism. Nor can we continue to keep passing ourselves off as the ultimate authority in private revelation.

We need to accept the fact that our human nature is prone to error, that none of us are infallible or without fault, and that we need Jesus, the Good Shepherd, to protect us.

The *Old Testament* merges into the *New Testament* with the book of *Malachi*. And the *New Testament* ends with the *Book of Revelation*. Interestingly, they both end with the same theme: The day of the coming of the Lord, "that great and terrible day." They end with a warning about adding or deleting anything from these books—about letting God be God.

Come, Lord Jesus!

CHAPTER 7

Conclusion

Jesus lives! He arose, and He ascended into Heaven. The gates have been opened for us and the victory is assured. We need only to do our part. The omnipotence of God is the only lasting power—the Alpha and the Omega. Only the Spirit of truth ultimately prevails, and God is truth. Without the Supreme Being mankind is doomed to eventually destroy itself, others and the environment. History has spelled it our for us over many centuries. All societies and governments have eventually crumbled. All major military powers have ultimately met defeat. Only His truth endures. His truth is in His Church. And it is in the only book that has withstood the test of time. It is called the **Bible**.

These are the tenets of our faith as passed on to us by His Church—and often confirmed by His Mother.

We live in extraordinary times. It is absolutely undeniable that there is dissension in the Church, that the world speeds headlong toward self-destruction and chastisement, and that apparitions and messages are being received everywhere warning us of these things, and how to prevent them.

But there is also a strong need to recognize the fact that neither Our Lady nor we individually are doing battle only with ourselves. There is an opposition in existence, and he is very real, a false angel of light. The battle between the Woman Clothed with the Sun and the red dragon is on, folks. It is happening now and the enemy is not always visible.

But the Lady's victory is also assured. It also is part of the Bible we hold so dear. The head of the serpent will be crushed. But until then, he can and does pursue the offspring of the New Adam and the New Eve with full vigor. He still has the opportunity to claim our soul. It would seem his time is very short. Perhaps ours as well. Here again, we need to do our part. Our salvation is guaranteed only if we do our part.

Perhaps private revelation, largely left to its own doing, has pushed us past what Our Lady and her Son are currently asking of us. Perhaps now we have decided it is in our control, that we have the answers, that we can defeat the red dragon on our own merits alone. We can't. Let God be God.

The United States, the greatest power on earth, along with the rest of the free world, spent seventy years trying to stave off the red menace and defeat atheistic Communism in the Soviet Union. During that period over 100 million people died at the hands of Communist oppression around the world. We never were able to totally stop it. Then, ten years ago or so, the Omnipotent God evidently gave a nod of His head, and it was instantly gone. And all the powers of the world stood dumbfounded, trying to explain it all in human terms.

With God all things are possible. The massive problems of the world and the Church require but a simple nod of His head for resolution. Jesus Christ told us that emphatically— that only He can give true peace. I guess then, that Our Lady's recommendations, "*Pray, pray, pray*," pretty much says it all. That prayer must be for every visionary in the world, for guidance and direction. It must be for every bishop and priest, and brother, and nun, especially for those who have so much difficulty with their vocation and who are being deluded by that evil spirit, the father of all lies and delusion.

At the same time, we need to be present and vocal and visible in our faith. If that is not a requirement, then why did Our Lord bother to send the Holy Spirit to empower the Apostles, to send them out to preach, and to build the body of the Church? And in our daily lives, and in our day to day activities of trying to seek out the Lord and in trying to respond to the requests of His Mother, we need to discern.

So why are we always trying to out-guess Him? Out-fox the Holy Spirit? Conquer it all with great technology? Why do we feel we suddenly need more doctrines or dogmas, or more revelation?

We've never been able to master the ones we were given to start with.

There may be a much greater need to pray for visionaries and special messengers than there is to go chasing after them. "Living the messages" may not entail visiting every apparition site that comes along, or accepting every message on face value alone. The color of your rosary is not as important as whether you pray with it, and the recognition that Christ physically comes to us every day in every Mass is more important than any sign in the sky. Maybe we need to worry less about our physical chastisement and more about the state of our souls, and how we get to where HE is.

Chastisement? Purification? End times? What are we going to do about it anyway? Are we actually going to respond in some way? Hopefully so. But how? Move to a refuge center? Store food and water? Get out of the stock market? Or is it just the case of wanting to read the latest message book? Some new sensational revelation, or some new theory on how and when it is all going to come down?

How about if we all just pay attention to that word mentioned earlier, the one that is always there—**conversion**? What would happen if everyone simply did that; if we all actually turned our lives over to God and paid attention to His call to come to His Divine Mercy, to seek love and forgiveness and simplicity of life?

"Unity?" I wonder if we can ever achieve it with the Orthodox Churches if we can't achieve it within the Roman Catholic Church?

There also seems little doubt that the ordained Church bears some of the responsibility for this sudden surge by so many toward claimed apparitions and messages. If spiritual needs are not being met from the pulpit, people will go somewhere else where they will be. Fortunately, I can attest to the fact that that is just not me talking. When you receive between 100 and 200 letters and phone calls a day, for a number of years, you get a pretty good feel for what the people are saying and experiencing all across the country. And what they are experiencing is neglect, and watered down Catholicism, or worse.

The rest of the bad news is that Satan can have a field day in that type of situation. And he apparently is. Evidently Lucifer can and does come as an "angel of light" and can draw many people into following apparently good messages with the intent of blowing the whole thing up somewhere down the road.

We live in exciting times. Maybe even perilous times. All the same, the Church will continue, as will the faith. But the simple fact of the matter is this:

> It seems the current Marian Movement and devotion is the most important, and strongest force in the Church today. It is also very evident that the Holy Father believes it as well. So does one other being, and Satan is as real as you and I, and he cannot afford to let it succeed. We desperately need to police ourselves, our ministries, our own profession, and as needed, each other.
>
> Greed, ego, fame, publicity, status, money, are all just human elements that eventually devour us. So is a false spirituality provided by Satan that can lead us to believe we are doing a great work for God by being one of His special prophets. It then gives birth to the first six elements listed above. And it is happening now.

Whether you receive material from the Riehle Foundation, or from anywhere else, discern. It is your responsibility to do so. If you are comfortable with it, if it brings you peace and directs you back to the Sacraments, if it increases your faith, hang on to it. If it brings you turmoil, doubt, or an uneasy feeling, drop it like a hot coal. That has been mentioned several times in this book.

Recognize that the New Age Movement is more than a myth. Satan attempts to mimic or copy EVERYTHING the Lord has given us—especially private revelation and mystical experiences. Channeling is not OK. Tai Chi is part of the New Age religion, and *A Course in Miracles* is not a Catholic book.

We all need to be more aware of those types of examples in our lives. Can we not best counteract these intrusions by returning to the basics of our faith? Make Jesus the first priority in your life. Consecrate your life to His most Sacred Heart, and to her Immaculate Heart. And then, **let God be God!**

Your only real chastisement can come if you refuse to accept the Divine Mercy as brought to us through Blessed Sister Faustina. Devotion to the Divine Mercy pretty well covers it all. He gave us the secret to our success—and our salvation—with one prayer:

Jesus, I Trust in You!

And as to the Marian movement, and devotion to Mary and the following of private revelation? Maybe there is a need to take another look at the Legion of Mary.

All of those ladies who have carried out the objectives of the Legion for the last seventy-five years? I think they had it right all along.

APPENDIX I

PRIVATE REVELATIONS
Suggested Rules for Discernment

It should be noted that the following criteria were taken from mystical theology treatises which have been in the Church for many years. It would seem that the explosion of apparitions in this century, and the position of the current Church with respect to private revelation, might indicate a need to further define or alter some of these suggested principles of the earlier Church. The following material was taken from: *The Spiritual Life* by Adolphe Tanquerey S.S., D.D., and *The Graces of Interior Prayer* by A. Poulain, S.J.

THE MANNER IN WHICH REVELATIONS ARE MADE

1) Visions (Apparitions);
2) Supernatural Words (Locutions);
3) Divine Touches (Charisms);

VISIONS are supernatural perceptions of some object naturally invisible to man. They are of three kinds:

a) Sensible or corporeal: where the senses actually perceive;
b) Imaginative: produced in the imagination by the supernatural, either during sleep or while awake;
c) Intellectual visions: where the mind perceives a spiritual truth without the aid of the senses.

SUPERNATURAL WORDS are manifestations of divine thought conveyed to the exterior or to the interior senses, or directly to the intelligence.

DIVINE TOUCHES are spiritual sentiments of goodness impressed upon the will.

RULES FOR THE DISCERNMENT OF REVELATIONS

Concerning the subject and object of the revelation:

1) Is the person well-balanced or affected by hysteria or emotional outbursts?
2) Is the person in possession of common sense and sound judgment, as opposed to a vivid imagination?
3) Is the person thoroughly sincere as opposed to having the habit of exaggerating?
4) Does the person have solid and tried virtue and a sense of sincere and deep humility?
5) Does the person take the revelation to a spiritual director and follow the lead of the Church?
6) Is the revelation in opposition to any truth of faith?
7) Is it opposed to any moral law?
8) Does it demand the impossible of the seer?

FIVE CAUSES OF POTENTIAL ERROR THAT CAN INFLUENCE PRIVATE REVELATIONS

1) Faulty interpretations of the message or vision by the visionary;
2) Ignorance of the fact that historic events are often given with approximate truth only;
3) The mingling of human activity with supernatural action during the revelation;
4) A subsequent, but involuntary, modification of the message made by the visionary;
5) Embellishments made by secretaries or compilers of the material.

FIVE POTENTIAL CAUSES THAT SHOW A PRIVATE REVELATION IS NOT AUTHENTIC

1) Simulation: Being untruthful as to the even or message;
2) An over-active mind or imagination;

3) The illusion of the memory: leads us to believe in events that never happened;
4) An action by Satan;
5) The inventions of falsifiers: Either by the visionary involved, or by associated individuals who seek some personal, public or political gain, or notoriety connected to the event.

Additional notes on:

False prophets: They do not allow themselves to be easily discouraged by their repeated failures. They always find some good reason to explain them away, or they pretend that the event is only delayed! When necessary, they proceed to confirm their first prophecy by some new revelation.

False locutions: There is a strange confusion between the "imagination," which constructs a scene, and the "memory," which affirms that it took place. Reason no longer distinguishes between these two very different operations.

APPENDIX II

(The following material is part of a document written by Fr. Rene Laurentin for the National Marian Conference at Notre Dame, May, 1989, and which was published by The Riehle Foundation).

The Criteria of the Church

Due to fundamental difficulties, Cardinal Seper published, on February 25, 1978, a concise four-page document entitled:

> *Normae Congregationis pro Doctrina Fidei de modo procedendi in diudicandis praesumptis apparitionibus ac revelationibus* ("Norms of the Holy Congregation for the teaching of the Faith concerning the procedure for judging presumed apparitions and revelations").

The Congregation of the Faith sends it to bishops who have to pass judgment on apparitions or private revelations. For this reason, the document is rather widely known today.

The document notes, first of all, that reports of apparitions spread very rapidly at the present time. In light of this, the bishop must very rapidly make a pronouncement, which will give them the green light or put a stop to them, by declaring:

> Certification of supernaturality, or Non-certification of supernaturality.

Here the document does not mention the very important variant which makes it possible to differentiate between negative judgments, i.e. the distinction between:

- <u>Non-certification</u> of supernaturality (the super naturality has not been established) and
- Certification of <u>non-supernaturality</u> (the non-supernaturality has been established).

The first form expresses a doubt but leaves the question open: the supernatural quality has not yet been established. The second excludes the supernatural and closes the question.

In Medjugorje, Bishop Zanic, who had collected (in a purely private way and without a vote) the opinions of the members of his Commission, before dissolving it as requested by Cardinal Ratzinger, had transformed the "non-certification of supernaturality" (which left the question open) into a "certification of non-supernaturality" (an exclusive negation). Certain members of the Commission objected to this abusive interpretation.

This same preamble recommends being attentive to the fruits of the apparitions, in accord with Christ's own criterion in the Gospel: *Judge the tree by its fruit* (*Matt.* 7:16-19).

The First Part:

The section (pg. 2-3), is entitled: Criteria to judge, at least with probability, the nature of presumed apparitions and revelations.

The document distinguishes successively:

A. Positive criteria
 1. Moral certainty, or at least great probability, of the existence of the fact, established by means of a serious investigation.

2. Particular circumstances bearing on the existence and nature of the fact, i.e.
   —Personal quality of the subject or subjects (especially, mental equilibrium, honesty and moral attitude, sincerity and habitual submission to ecclesiastical authority, ability to return to the regime of normal faith (i.e. life without visions).
   —From the point of view of the revelation: theological and spiritual doctrine true and free from error.
   —Sound devotion and rich spiritual fruits which last: for example, spirit of prayer, conversions, signs of charity.

B. Negative criteria
   1. Determine error as to the facts.
   2. Doctrinal error (. . .) taking into account the possibility that the subject may unconsciously add human elements to authentic supernatural revelation. (Saint Ignatius, Exercises, No. 336).
   3. Evident seeking of financial advantage, directly connected with the fact.
   4. Seriously immoral acts, at the time or on the occasion of the fact, committed by the subject (the seer) and his acolytes.
   5. Fifth negative criterion is mental illness and psychopathic tendencies on the part of the subject, or psychosis or collective hysteria and diseases of this kind.

It should be noted that these criteria, either positive or negative, are indicative and not absolute and must be taken cumulatively as they converge.

The Second Part:

The document from the *Congregation of the Faith* details how competent ecclesiastical authority is to proceed.

In short:
A. The authority (residing bishop) has the grave duty of finding out about, and keeping an eye on these presumed supernatural facts.
B. At the request of the faithful, the authority may foster

forms of worship and devotion related to the event, but it is important that this not be considered by the faithful as an approval of the apparitions.

C. By virtue of his doctrinal and pastoral authority, the competent authority can and should intervene on his own initiative in certain circumstances. For example, to correct or prevent abuses in devotion, to condemn false doctrine, to avoid the dangers of a false and harmful mysticism, etc.

D. In doubtful cases, which do not involve the welfare of the Church, the ecclesiastical authority may refrain from any judgment or direct action but the authority must keep an eye out so that, if necessary, it can intervene rapidly and prudently.

The Third Part

The authority competent to intervene confirms that such authority belongs to the local Ordinary.

But it adds (and this is new):

The regional or national Conference of Bishops may intervene, either at the request of the local Ordinary or because the event assumes national or regional importance.

Finally the Apostolic See (Rome) can intervene:

—at the request of the Ordinary himself
—or of a qualified group of the faithful,
—or directly, by virtue of the universal jurisdiction of the Sovereign Pontiff.

The Fourth and Last Part:

The Seper Document concludes with:

A. Concerning the involvement of the Congregation for the Teaching of the Faith—who may take the initiative?

1. The involvement of the Sacred Congregation may be requested:

—Either by the Ordinary, after he has completed his work

—Or by qualified groups of the faithful (again, experts).

In this latter case, care must be taken so that the Sacred Congregation is not called on for questionable reasons, such as in order to force the Ordinary to change his legitimate decisions, or to confirm some sectarian group, etc.

2. The Sacred Congregation has the right to become involved on its own initiative in the most serious cases, especially if the event affects a larger part of the Church.

The document adds: This involvement will always take place in consultation with the Ordinary and, if need be, the Conference of Bishops.

It is the prerogative of the Sacred Congregation:

—Either to approve what the Ordinary has done (i.e. the bishop)

—Or to institute a new investigation, separate from the one carried out by the Ordinary. (This is the case in Medjugorje where Cardinal Ratzinger entrusted the Conference of Bishops with this new investigation)

—Or to make the judgment itself, or through a special Commission.

This last part of the Constitution provides for new possibilities of action by the Holy See. Prior to this, in practice, Rome normally used a maximum of discretion.

The Significance Of
The Church's Approval

Two Stages

1. Recognition of the devotions (first stage)

"If the investigation produces a favorable result, ecclesiastical authority may permit certain forms of public worship or devotions, over which it will keep a very careful watch. This amounts to saying: for the time being, nihil obstat, there is nothing against the devotion" "(Criteria of the Congregation of the Faith, February 25, 1978, pg. 1-2).

2. Recognition of the apparitions

"With the light that time and experience may shed (especially the spiritual fruit produced by the new devotion), a judgment can be made as to the truth and supernatural character of the apparitions (ibid. 1978, pg. 2).

Cardinal Lambertini, the future Benedict XIV, whose book, *De Servorum Dei Canonizatione et Beatificatione* has been considered authoritative since its publication in the 18th century, declared clearly:

"The approval given by the Church to a private revelation is nothing else than the permission accorded after careful examination, to publish this revelation for the instruction and the good of the faithful. Even if they are approved by the Church one must **not** and one cannot grant the assent of Catholic Faith to such revelations.
"In keeping with laws of prudence, one must give them only the assent of human belief, in that such revelations are probable and piously credible. Consequently it is possible to refuse to accept such revelations and to turn from them, as long as

DEAR MARION MOVEMENT

one does so with proper modesty, for good reasons, and without the intention of setting himself up as superior." (*De Servorum Dei Beatificatione*, Book 2, Chapter 32, No. 11; cf. also Book 3, Chapter 53, No. 15).

Pius X confirms this position in his encyclical Pascendi, September 8, 1907:

"The Church uses such prudence that it does not allow apparitions to be reported in the press, except with great caution, and after insertion of the statement required by Urban VIII. Even in this case of official recognition, it does not guarantee the truth of the fact. It simply does not oppose believing things for which reasons of human faith are not lacking." (*Actes de Pie X, Paris, Bonne Presse*, T. 3, pg. 175).

Attitude Which The Church Requires Of The Faithful

In keeping with its finality and its mission, the church requires adherence to two basic policies regarding apparitions or similar phenomena.

1. A FIRM FAITH, OPEN TO THE LIVING COMMUNICATIONS OF THE LIVING GOD.

   This is very important for the vitality of the Church. Faithful who act only as required by juridical obedience, without reaching out, without initiative, without living reference to the living God, possess a dead faith and make up a dead Church. Wherever the Church is alive (as twenty centuries of history have shown), the faithful, who believe in Christ, in the Virgin and the Saints, desire to meet them, to communicate with them. This is done through prayer, the sacraments, and other avenues of grace. If there are reasons to think that Christ or the Virgin are coming and speaking, how can one remain indifferent? It is therefore normal that the faithful seek to know more, when apparitions happen under serious circumstances, and that they go on pilgrimage to the site.

2. PRUDENCE, HUMILITY, OBEDIENCE TO AUTHORITY, RESPECT OF OTHERS, AND CHARITY.

   The faithful (and authority itself!) are not infallible in this conjectural matter. They must therefore be vigilant, careful to avoid the snares of illusion or of illuminism.

Consequently:
—They should make their judgement with prudence; carefully verify the facts. They must show critical and self-critical sense, i.e. discernment.
—In addition, they should consider the good order of the Church, and avoid the excessive emotion and

disorder which might be caused by enthusiasm for apparitions.

—They must even take care not to cause scandal or disorder. They must use intelligence, prudence, measure, and discretion in publishing the messages, for example.

—Last (but not least), they must be constantly respectful and obedient in respect to the authority of the church.

It should be noted here that all of these guidelines could be mute points, if in fact the claimed apparitions and/or messages are based on one or more of the following criteria:

—Messages, actions, or statements contrary to the teachings or accepted practices of the Church.

—Un-truths, deceptions, or activity which tends to bring scandal to the Church.

—An apparent attempt to gain profit or other economic benefits, or status, position, publicity, for personal use.

(These last three items are not the words of Fr. Laurentin but are included by the author of this book as derived from a number of other guidelines regarding the discernment of private revelation).

APPENDIX III

Current Visionaries, Locutionists, and Apparition Sites

The following is a list of some of the more recognizable sites or messengers of the past fifteen to twenty years. It is not meant to ridicule, support, approve, or disprove any one or any site. It is merely a reflection of the enormous amount of material currently available regarding claimed messages from the Heavenlies through private revelation.

Internationally

Aside from the widely known events of Medjugorje, there have been major phenomena and messages at Marmora, Canada; Nicaragua; Kibeho, Africa (several of the seers have been killed); The Phillipines; Ukraine; England and many parts of Ireland; Damascus; a number of claimed apparitions in Buddhist and Muslim areas; South America; Hindu area of India; several in Australia. Recognized names of seers affiliated with these sites would include:

Wladyslaw Biernacki

Georgette Faniel

Sr. Guadalupe

Gladys Quiorga De Motta

Patricia (England)
Bernardo Martinez
Josefina (Australia)
Matthew Kelly
Jim Singer
Pachi (Ecuador)
Emma de Guzman

Vassula Ryden
Maria Esperanza
Christine Gallagher
Julia Kim
Sr. Marie Danielle
Mirna (Damascus)
Debra (Australia)

United States

The United States now provides a wide array of claimed locations for supernatural visitations, refuge centers, promotions for new shrines, apparitions, new centers, and sites of mystical powers such as healing springs. Far too much space would be required to detail all of these locations and/or what is supposedly taking place there. We limit our list to only the more generally known:

St. Maria Goretti Church
Apostolatus Uniti
Marlboro, NJ
Tri-State (OH, IN, KY)
Bella Vista, AR (now TX)
Chicago, IL
Santa Maria, CA
St. Mary's, Ohio
Akron, OH

Mother Cabrini Shrine (CO)
Lubbock, Texas
Hollywood, FL
Conyers, GA
Bloomington, IN
Medway, MA
Refuge Centers (Kucera)
Marantha Spring
    (Cleveland, OH)

In addition to the above locations, some of the major messengers of messages in the United States would include the following. The names shown are all known and publically used and identified in materials distributed. A partial list:

Augustine Halvorsen
Mary Constancio & Mike Slate
Fran & Steve Wise
Tracey Giroux
Rita Ring
Batavia Visionary
Maureen Sweeney
Peter Gruters
Theresa Werner
Robt Hartmann
Janie Garza
The Scribe

Sr. Margaret Sims

Vincent Bemowski
Fr. Edward Carter
Charlene Huber
Pat MacDonald
Tony Fernwalt
Al Solis
Little Billy
Dorothy Romano
Marv Kucera
Roger King

Lori
Steve Marino
Danny Mohn
Carol Ameche
Barbara Matthias
Carlos Lopez & Jorge
Estela Ruiz
Joe Januszkiewicz
Nancy Fowler
Josyp Terelya
Denise Morgan-Estrada
Veronica Garcia
Sadie Jarmillo
Joseph Reinholtz
Lena Shipley
Sharon Witton
Sandy

Mariamante
Rosa Lopez
Mary's Messenger
Lorna Keras
Carol Nole
Jan Connell
Gianna Sullivan
Cyndi Cain
Theresa Lopez
Louise Lahola
Mary Jane Even
Annie Ross-Fitch
Ruth Ann Wade
Raymond Shaw
Diane Rodgers
Joanne Kriva
Maria Paula

There are an additional thirty to forty names of messengers that could be added to this list. However, I do not know if all of their material, and/or their names have been made public.

Discernment: A Needed Grace, Especially in America

It is more than just some uneasy feeling about something you are reading or viewing. It is more than just listening to someone else's doubts. It requires questioning on your part, seeking answers for those uneasy feelings, getting clarification on those troublesome aspects of messages and prophecies, instead of just seeking out all the good, fluffy stuff and ignoring the rest.

The following pages use several different messengers and apparition sites in the United States as examples. These examples are used in that the potential problems, or existing problems, are already known or have been documented through others. As previously stated, defining and answering these questions will still not authenticate or disprove any claimed visionary, but it might provide a lot of assistance in getting rid of those uneasy feelings or doubts that many of us have—and should have.

Warning signs become apparent. In some cases they seem like an occasional red flag. In other cases a constant flashing red light. And it is not, and should not, just be our personal reflection on the visionary involved. It seems to be getting more and more complex and there are increasing indications that mystics can be and are used by others for the wrong reasons. Some specific situations follow. They are examples of some current difficulties, not an attempt to support or diminish someone's spirituality or messages she or he claims to be receiving.

Specific Examples

Mary Jane Even and Vassula were noted earlier in this book, and the sanctions levied against them by the Church. In Mary Jane Even's case, the messages were at times so bizarre that extensive discernment didn't even seem necessary.

Vassula's story is much more complex, and probably not finished yet. Concerns over "automatic writing" and "channeling" (prime tools in the New Age Movement), questionable aspects of unity and intermingling of Orthodox and Catholic doctrines, confusing theology, all allowed for the Holy See to take some position in the matter. Others took a more personal view, citing Vassula's "look like Jesus appearance," or her ability to seemingly mesmerize a following. It then expanded across continents. Other visionaries and organizations became intertwined. Perhaps that was not in their best interest—or Vassula's.

The negative action of the Vatican ignited responses from individuals and apostolates that shouldn't have taken place, casting a wider and longer shadow in the process. People (including priests) were choosing up sides—for or against the Church's position. Included was Dr. and Claire Mansour from California who had originally strongly supported Mirna (from Damascus). At one point or another, a number of seers or apostolates seemed to be linked to Vassula and to each other. Included were Mirna, Theresa Lopez, Vassula, King of All Nations, the 101 Foundation, and a visionary from Australia named Debra.

Mirna might be an example to show the need to discern intentions of promoters and publishers more than the messages, but in any case, the example shows us the far reaching scope of the results.

How much injury to these apostolates or seers was created

with the release of certain sanctions by the Church regarding Vassula? Or, has support for Vassula from any of these apostolates or seers done more harm than good—including to themselves? To add to the consternation, a phone call from an apostolate in Australia (July 23, 1996), indicated a bishop there had issued a negative statement regarding the seer, Debra. Concerns that could use answers.

American Apparition Sites

I became acquainted with Carol Nole, a visionary from Santa Maria, California, approximately six years ago. She is a very humble, sincere and spiritual lady. The messages there involved the requested construction of a large cross in the Santa Maria area (the Cross of Peace project). A second visionary surfaced. Dissension. Two camps were formed. The spiritual director, Monsignor John Rhode, switched sides and went with the second seer. The group supporting her solicited Fr. René Laurentin to write a book supporting her and set up special testings to confirm her ecstasies.

Additional seers surfaced (as always). Messages of doom and impending natural disasters became common. (Interestingly, in 1993, Msgr. Rhode had issued a request not to have Nancy Fowler, Denise Morgan and Louise Lahola as speakers at a planned anniversary celebration and conference because of the apocalyptic nature of their messages.) The second seer, Barbara Matthias, was endorsed in the book by Fr. Laurentin and is now titled "the most tested visionary in the history of the Church" (but not approved). Further credibility was sought by bringing a visionary from Scottsdale to California for the same testing. She initially refused, citing advice from the Virgin Mary, but under some apparent heavy pressure, finally relented. Most of the prophecies from Santa Maria have been wrong and there is documentation that does not agree with materials made available regarding Barbara.

Conyers, Georgia, is a familiar apparition site to anyone acquainted with American reported phenomena, and Nancy Fowler has attracted a very large following. Many books and videos have been produced covering her story and her messages. Her messages, along with those of Cyndi Cain, are extremely apocalyptic. Most of the prophecies, at least to this point, have not been correct. Apparently, there are many who question the contradictions within Nancy's messages. Examples would include:

There is no reparation anywhere in the world. . . . The Fatima consecration requested by the Blessed Virgin Mary has **not** been done. . . . You are wrong to seek signs and wonders. . . . Signs and wonders will be experienced here like nowhere else. . . . Satan is deceiving you by false messages. . . . People must accept you. . . . The Church must recognize Nancy, or else. . . . All visionaries should test. . . . Stop all this testing. . . . The world has rejected the Blessed Virgin Mary because they don't come to Conyers. . . . etc.

An article in *Crisis Magazine* provided an excellent critique on the Conyers events, including restrictions placed by former Bishop, James Lyke. Some of those have since been clarified, but the current Archbishop, John F. Donoghue, has not taken any further action. Additional questions that apparently surfaced included why she is building a bomb shelter in her basement, stocked with food, and whether she has any emotional illness. I have no knowledge or concern with any of that. But on the one hand, the extensive publicity given to Nancy's testing episodes included an evaluation from a noted psychiatrist stating no abnormalities anywhere. On the other hand, a major article in the Atlanta newspaper, *The Constitution*, included extensive accounts from former workers for Nancy who testified that she was often in depression, in emotional stress, and often saw demons everywhere. There was also another report that prior to the start of her apparitions she experienced poltergeist activity in her home and once saw a UFO land on her property. Is that the case? Interestingly, many people who have gone to Conyers report very positive experiences, and there are accounts of spiritual and physical healings. Solar phenomena and strange photos, along with rosaries changing color are often reported. It becomes a good example of the difficulties encountered in private revelation, and more importantly, of the need to recognize at least the potential for false messages caused by the wrong spirits. The positive aspects always speak for themselves and are avidly promoted. The negative is sometimes ignored.

Perhaps two of the most interesting examples of the need for discernment in private revelation would be Bella Vista,

Arkansas, where the visionary was Cyndi Cain, and the events in Cincinnati/Northern Kentucky, where a handful of claimed visionaries are involved. Most of this is already known in many circles, since there are many volumes of books and tapes available concerning these events. It provides an excellent example of the potential pitfalls we face, and the prayers and discernment we all need to utilize on a daily basis, not only for ourselves, but for the participants in these events as well.

Cyndi's ministry suddenly came upon the Arkansas scene after a sojourn on the West Coast. The new location was apparently the result of a direct request from Our Lady. Cyndi and her husband, Michael, are both writers. That is evidenced by the appeal of their *Call to Peace* publication and the depth of the articles. The initial area of discernment regarding Cyndi's ministry would be the messages themselves. Since there were often four or more messages per week, going back to 1990, there is a mammoth amount of words from Jesus and Mary to read. These are generally more apocalyptic than even the Conyers messages and are usually presented in the form of specific prophecy stated by Jesus. A first problem is, most of it has been wrong, and as is often the case, much of it contradicts itself, or in some cases, the Church. Some examples might include: The beginning of the chastisements was in February of 1991. . . . The Gulf War was to go on as a prelude to world war and the appearance of the antichrist. . . . 1992 was to be the time of the great schism in the Church (confirmed by Nancy Fowler), and that year the United States was also to come to doom (the land shall be ravaged, the economy will collapse. Aug. 1992). . . . Woe to anybody who doubts a seer. . . . These are the last days, now counted in hours (Sept. 92). . . . Now is the secret of Fatima fulfilled (Dec. 92). . . . etc.

Additional messages stated these are the last days (Sept. 93) and the angel of light had now marked the forehead of those who would remain faithful. Evidently that was those who agreed to move to the refuges. Jesus stated all churches must be opened 24 hours a day, Eucharist in the hand is an abomination, and the Blessed Sacrament must be led in procession to every abortion clinic. Cyndi also announced specific messages had been received for the instigation of a special refuge center and a new order of nuns. It would seem there is a need for the laity to be able to better identify these kinds of messages—preferably by having the Church issue some sort of statement relating thereto—before we get too excited and donate money, or even move our families. Such seems to be the case here. Messages in 1992 confirmed Cyndi and Michael were to travel to Rome for a special audience with the Pope confirming the new order to be established in Arkansas, who was to run it, that the Pope would personally endorse it, that it would be a "Eucharistic Community" (the Blessed Sacrament always available—but not approved by the local bishop), that the Pope would be martyred in Denver in 1993, the realization of the location for the new refuge and holy Monastery; the appointment (by Our Lady) of special hand picked sons and daughters to administer these operations. Donations were to be solicited for the refuge center and a call for people to come there, through the publication, *A Call to Peace.*

For whatever reason, almost all of the predictions turned out to be wrong and by 1994, many Marian organizations around the country were receiving letters from residents of the Bella Vista Refuge indicating major problems, a lack of confidence in Cyndi, and suggesting people not come. Messages from Our Lady (or Jesus) were provided for every situation, problem, or decision to be made, including identifying the property to be purchased (it was the wrong one); a religious to be the head of the new order (as it turned out she evidently wasn't a nun); a Brother Anthony, picked by Our Lady to then head up the order (turned out he really wasn't a Brother. There was a Brother Anthony associated with a claimed Bishop Konstantinos in Cincinnati. Is there some connection there?)

The refuge failed, money was lost, a spiritual director left, an investigation was initiated by the Chancery, litigation was threatened, families left the center, and the Cains left the state. The *Call to Peace* newspaper deftly reported the entire array of difficulties and pointed out the reality of Satan in the process, and how it was he who had infiltrated and destroyed this otherwise good work.

And why couldn't that be the case?

Regardless, detailing some of those difficulties is presented here that all might benefit from them, not to expose someone else's plight. In that vein, I think there is a special need for all of us to question those situations where a visionary can come up with a message for every need, for any person who needs one, and at the spur of the moment anytime.

Several years ago, I had received a letter from Cyndi inviting us to publish a book for her, stating this request was given directly by the Blessed Virgin Mary. I have received quite a few such requests, and once, when I refused, I was told I now had "blood on my hands." I don't think so.

In early 1992, a visionary surfaced in the Cincinnati area, to be known as "The Batavia Visionary." She predicted a great appearance by the Blessed Virgin Mary to take place in Cold Spring, Kentucky, at a Catholic Church there. The scheduled event was heavily promoted in the media and gave rise to new apostolates and organizations to function in this special location of grace "planned by the Lord since the beginning of time." The seer eventually identified other priests who were supposedly hand picked by Our Lady to head this special new ministry, including and under the direction of Fr. Leroy Smith, pastor of the parish to which Our Lady was to appear. Other apparition sites and ministries were also evidently identified by Our Lady. A closed seminary was purchased as a special center, future retreat house, residence for priests, and to function as a Marian center for spirituality. Certainly a noble and worthy effort.

There may not be another location of claimed private revelation, anywhere in the country, that has a stronger base of committed and devoted Marian followers than the Southern Ohio-Northern Kentucky area which serves these claimed apparitions. I personally know many of them (Milford, Ohio is a suburb of Cincinnati), and there is a tremendous Catholic presence here, as well as a heavy commitment to the Mother of God. Obviously that indicates a need for special vigilance because adoration of the Lord, miracles, conversions and apparitions have a habit of drawing the wrong spirits into the picture as well.

The new ministries, as initiated at this site of alleged private revelation, were headed up by Fr. Smith and Gerald Ross, a dedicated layman, under the banner of "Our Lady of Light Publications." This has been expanded to other ministries and affiliations since 1993. Much of the detail regarding the story of this apparition site is covered in a number of publications by the *Our Lady of Light* network, and was the focal point of an issue of *Signs of the Times Magazine* as well. There may be a need to question some of the sequence of events as shown in those publications since there are some differences of opinion. A number of individuals have also seen fit to question a number of the messages that have surfaced since 1992.

One visionary suddenly became six visionaries. All seemed to be openly accepted and their messages and stories published accordingly. As is often the case, different groups formed, while more messages called for the start of additional new ministries. Real estate was now involved, and extensive donations were solicited. An additional visionary and messages included the request to purchase a farm. The Batavia Visionary, through Mary, related how the entire Tri-state area (Ohio-Kentucky-Indiana common borders) was to become the major center of renewal for the Church. Messages were received for specific priests and persons involved in ministry at the sites. More message books were published with the inevitable result that now division and confusion were setting in. Different factions drew different supporters.

At the height of the activity, Fr. Edward Carter, S.J., a member of the Priests' Board directing the events, and who was in unison with and advisor to certain of the visionaries, announced that he himself was now a locutionist, asked by the Lord to start a whole new configuration of ministries.

The good news was that this promoted supernatural activity was drawing many thousands of people to the Northern Kentucky/Cincinnati locations and many apparent good and positive fruits were noted. Prayer groups, liturgies, and special Marian devotions flourished. Many hundreds of people donated time, effort and finances for the refurbishing of the former seminary and the purchase and development of a farm property in Falmouth, Kentucky. Dayton, Ohio, claimed to be part of the Tri-State spiritual center, as well as properties in Indiana. The network became a very large and diverse network of ministries, publications—including newsletters, tapes, and a whole array of local visionary apparition books, outreach ministries and special devotional programs, workshops, seminars and speaking engagements held at the former seminary, now known as the **Our Lady of the Holy Spirit Center**.

The bad news is perhaps not even known yet in its entirety, but it certainly lends itself to some questions, particularly since the Church has yet to take an active position in the whole matter. The Bishop of the Diocese of Covington, Kentucky, did not take a particularly favorable view of the original predicted apparition at Cold Spring, Kentucky, and his new successor is probably not familiar enough with the entire matter to take any position at this point. The potential bad news aspects that do evoke questions, and that are known, apparently include:

- A need to question the quantity and quality of visionaries.
- There is apparently a lot of questionable theology, especially in *God's Blue Book*.
- It was reported some messages have been changed or deleted as a result.
- One seer received messages to have Cyndi Cain's messages included in the publications, and further, produced messages that seemed to pre-date or contradict messages of one of the local seers who has apparently decided not to become part of the network.
- The reading and distribution of messages has become of paramount importance and all decisions seem to be based on a visionary providing a supernatural message for direction.
- Seemingly, there are messages that need specific clarification, or that are not in keeping with Catholic Doctrine (such as "these messages are to be added to public revelation"), or that prompted questions of origin (the prayer/hymn, "Our Lady of Light," is also word for word on an old picture prayer card printed in Italy).
- The entire events were to be guided by a board of priests. However, at least four of them were themselves involved with messages from Our Lady directed to them, and one is himself a visionary. Thus there exists an almost impossible discernment difficulty.

New areas of concern surfaced in that messages received by Fr. Carter called for a whole new configuration of ministries and organizations. One such ministry, *Shepherds of Christ*, was specifically directed by Jesus to replace the international organization, *The Marian Movement of Priests* as founded by Fr. Stefano Gobbi. Financial donations were supposed to be diverted to this new ministry and a lay apostolate of chapters set up to provide support and financial aid. There may also be a need for all of us to be a little more concerned where those kind of messages are being received.

Also, messages that name other people or 3rd parties. In the above ministries, messages were received from Jesus appointing people to specific organizations, giving them titles, naming ministries or formulating new organizations, complete with subsidiaries. Messages were received that openly condemned others for not doing such and such or not supporting the claimed visionaries. Material is distributed directly by one visionary promoting her own books and messages under specific titles given to her by Jesus, and at His request. All happens at the direction of a message.

Power, fame, fortune, and ego are all a part of that many-headed monster produced by that false angel of light. And they certainly can come very cleverly disguised. Visionaries, with all of their good intentions, might need to question whether Jesus or Mary make those kinds of mistakes, produce that kind of division, give messages based on building empires or taking over other ministries, or condemning any other individual who doesn't go along with it.

One of the local visionaries involved didn't. She has refused to publish a "message book," or accept the premise of the above referenced organizations. That may well be to her credit. Attempts to curtail the reading and distribution of messages as a major function of activities in the tri-state area, in the face of so many that are questionable, has evidently not succeeded. Usage or development of the farm property causes further division. Is there something terribly wrong here? Or not?

In the midst of it all is the profound devotion and faith of the local people involved. Their efforts have restored a magnificent chapel in the purchased former seminary. There is a schedule of devotions there, week in and week out, that rivals the Vatican. Thousands respond. They claim "good fruits" for their response, and there are many witnesses who can speak of conversions, healing, a deeper sense of the reality of the Lord and the importance of His Mother. Such is the case with many apparition sites. The concern is not the initial fruits, but what happens when it all starts to unravel. Whether anything is unraveling in the tri-state area is for the Church and the people involved to determine. And I for one hope they do. Too many good people are in questionable position there.

It may be important for those involved to evaluate and further determine the importance of several contributing factors to the events since 1992. It was reported that Cyndi Cain was a major factor in the development of these apparitions in that she predicted them in 1991. That may not be so. She responded to a letter from the current Executive Director of these local organizations. Cyndi was formerly a resident of northern Kentucky and a former neighbor of some of these people. As is often the case with Cyndi, she provided a supernatural message for someone who was looking for one. One report surfaced that had Cyndi formerly a novice in a local convent here. Former residents of the refuge in Arkansas stated that she and the "Batavia Visionary" had conversed prior to the whole thing starting. Fr. Carter's ministry was predicated upon a message from Cyndi Cain, who confirmed his locutions were authentic. Other local visionaries also provided this confirmation. But no one has confirmed them, except each other. Messages from this group have been available to the local director to provide whatever "mystical support" was required for himself, Fr. Carter, Fr. Smith, Fr. Sweeney, Fr. Reinfret, or Fr. Kenney. Rita Ring, appointed by Jesus as National Coordinator in the *Shepherds of Christ* network, and author of *God's Blue Book*, which was openly endorsed by Fr. Carter, was known by and affiliated with him at Xavier University in Cincinnati. There may be a need to evaluate the importance of the fact that all of these people are intertwined and knew each other—before it all happened. Such is the case with other groups of seers and publishers in the United States.

Enough for examples. Let's go back to the positive side, and let's stay with the tri-state area events. Like many other such sites, there is an equal litany of positives. In the case of the Holy Spirit Center the list is very impressive, as noted earlier. It prompts obvious questions:

> Couldn't we just continue to offer praise and adoration to the Lord and provide devotion to His Mother without reading and distributing somebody's claimed messages? Is the response of so many, to the availability of the Sacrament of Confession, the Rosary prayer groups, the Sacrifice of the Mass, Adoration of the Blessed Sacrament, only viable because someone is claiming messages there? Could not that same commitment be present simply because the Lord has asked, is worthy, and has offered His life for our redemption? Couldn't we accomplish the same things but without the confusion, the division, the egos, the power struggles, the inflated mysticism? Do we actually believe God's grace is less available at a Mass that doesn't involve a visionary, or with a Rosary that is not prayed on some supposed hallowed ground?

The praise and adoration, the Sacraments, the graces, the peace and eternal hope are all **His** doing. All those other things and problems are our doing.

NOTES

NOTES: CHAPTER I

Much of the history of Marian devotion and the development of various prayers and sacramentals was obtained
from the book by Don Sharkey, *"The Woman Shall Conquer,"*
Franciscan Marytown Press, Libertyville, IL., also *"The
Rosary and Devotion to Mary,"* by Deacon Andrew Gerakas,
published by The Daughters of St. Paul, Boston, MA. *"Power
of the Rosary"* is published by The Riehle Foundation, Milford, OH.

One of the most complete treatments of Mary's role in the
Church is provided by the Pastoral Letter of the National
Conference of Catholic Bishops titled: *"Behold Your Mother:
Woman of Faith,"* 1973. It is recommended. Defense of Mary
in the first centuries of the Church was taken from the book
by Veralyn Alpha, *"A Heavenly Journey,"* published by Faith
Publishing Company, Milford, OH. Specific quotations pertaining to the Church's position on Mary as defined by Vatican II can be found in the book, *"Vatican II—Marian
Council"* by Prof. William G. Most, also published by The
Daughters of St. Paul. The *Legion of Mary Handbook* was
published by the Legion in Dublin, Ireland, in 1969. It is not
known if it is still in print.

NOTES: CHAPTER II

The book, *"Behold Your Mother,"* is the pastoral produced

by the National Conference of Catholic Bishops, Washington, DC. References to specific segments of the Vatican Council document, "*Constitution on the Church*," were produced by the Daughters of St. Paul, as noted in previous chapter. Additional data concerning the Council was taken from "*The Woman Shall Conquer*" by Don Sharkey, Franciscan Marytown Press, Libertyville, IL. References to Church Canons, Doctrines and guidelines pertaining to apparitions and publications pertaining thereto were taken from the booklet, "*The Church and Apparitions*" by Rev. René Laurentin, published by The Riehle Foundation, Milford, Ohio. Quotation from Rev. Burt Buby was taken from an article in "*Our Sunday Visitor*," July, 1994. Titles and exhortations given to Mary were taken from the book, "*Mary, Mother of the Church*," published by TAN Books and Publishers, Rockford, IL. Other material from Fr. Bertrand Buby was taken from the article, "Mary's Real Presence in the World."

NOTES: CHAPTER III

Graces of Interior Prayer, by Fr. A. Poulain, and *The Three Ages of the Interior Life*, by Fr. R. Garrigou-LaGrange, are excellent treatises on private revelation used throughout this book. They go back many years and were published by the B. Herder Book Company, St. Louis, MO. Father J. Michael Miller's book, *Marian Apparitions and the Church*, is published by OSV Press, Huntington, IN. The article by Stacy Mattingly, "Reports of Mary," appeared in the November, 1995 issue of *Crisis Magazine*.

Fr. Bertrand Buby's statements appeared in an interview in *Our Sunday Visitor*, July 31, 1995, titled "Mary's Real Presence in the World." The article dealing with the reality of Satan and evil appeared in the November 13, 1995 issue of *Newsweek*. *The Ratzinger Report*, a highly recommended book on the status of the Church, is published by Ignatius Press. The material provided by Fr. René Laurentin, and the data covering the Church's criteria for the judging of apparitions is taken from Fr. Laurentin's booklet, *The Church and Apparitions*, originally published by The Riehle Foundation.

Throughout this book, material has been pulled from a previous work of this author titled, *Thoughts*, published by The Riehle Foundation. Fr. Albert J. Hebert's book, *The Dis-*

cernment of Visionaries and Apparitions Today, is published by, and available from the author, P.O. Box 309, Paulina, LA. 70763. *Medjugorje, A Closer Look* was written by Rev. Vittorio Guerrera, and published by Maryheart Crusaders Inc., Meriden, CT.

The documents of Vatican II, as cited earlier are available from a number of sources including The Daughters of St. Paul. The *Code of Canon Law* can be acquired from the *Canon Law Society of America*, Washington, DC. 20064.

The *New Catechism of the Catholic Church* is published by a number of sources including, The Wanderer Newspaper, St. Ignatius Press, Ligouri Publications, and the United States Bishop Conference, Publications Division.

NOTES: CHAPTER IV

Material pertaining to specific visionaries or messengers, and the messages distributed in their behalf is taken directly from books and tapes produced by those involved, or from other publications and apostolates which produced story lines or interviews with those involved, and which would include the following: **Our Lady of Light Foundation** and **Shepherds of Christ Ministries**, regarding events in Ohio and Northern Kentucky, and including the books *Personal Revelations of Our Lady of Light* and *God's Blue Book*. Other references include: *Messages of Love* by Veronica Garcia; *The Messages to The Churches* by Vincent Bemowski. *The Discernment of Visionaries and Apparitions Today* by Fr. Albert Hebert, S.M.; *Mary: Coredemptrix, Mediatrix, Advocate* by Dr. Mark Miravalle, *Thoughts* by William A. Reck; *All Powerful is the Name of The Lord*, By Lorna Keras; *When God Gives a Sign* (Vassula) by Fr. René Laurentin; *Our Holy Mother of Virtues* (Theresa Lopez); *In the Kingdom of the Spirit* by Josyp Terelya; *Lessons from Jesus* by Louise Lahola; *As We Wait in Joyful Hope* by Carol Ameche; *My Heart Awaits You* (several volumes) by Marvin Kucera; *The Miracle of Damascus* by The Publican; *The Glory of God* by Joanne Kriva, *Holy Love* (messages to seer in Cleveland) by Our Lady's Foundation, *Apparitions of the Virgin Mary* by Tony Fernwalt; *I Have Come to Set the Earth on Fire* by Dorothy Romano; *The Thunder of Justice* by Ted and Maureen Flynn.

Also included: *Z'Atelier Publications*; *Signs of the Times Magazine* (a quantity of interviews and stories on visionaries); **Queenship Publishing** (new Miraculous Medal) **Dr. Mary Jane Even** (many booklets, seer opposed by Church); **A Call to Peace** (publication by Cyndi and Michael Cain); *March for Love, Heaven is on the Move*, (one of a number of volumes by claimed seer Peter Gruters); **United for the Triumph of the Immaculate Heart** (Apostolate of Bishop Hnilica); **The 101 Foundation** (publisher); **The Marian Movement of Priests** (Fr. Stefano Gobbi); *Jesus King of All Nations Devotion Inc.*; **Catholic Commentary** (publication) by Steve Mahowald; *Our Loving Mother's Children* (publication of messages to Nancy Fowler, Conyers, GA); **Crisis Magazine** ("Reports of Mary" article, Nov. 95); **Our Lady Queen of Peace** (publication-newspaper) by Tom Petrisko.

Also included: **Mary's People** (newspaper supplement of Nat'l Catholic Register); *Mother of the Eucharist and Grace* (Philippine apparitions of Carmelo Cartez); **Faithful and True of the Midwest** (publication connected with Andrew Wingate—claimed seer known as "The Trumpeter," and also "The Little Pebble"); **The Cross of Peace** (apostolate in Santa Maria involving visionary Carol Nole); *The Book of the True Life* by Three Era's Inc.; *Overview of the New Age Movement* by William Reck (New Age incorporation of apparitions and messages); **Gospa Missions** (publication of Thomas Rutkoski); **End Times Apostles in Colorado** (apostolate—true photo of Jesus critics); *The Way of the Cross in Santa Maria* by Fr. René Laurentin (the seer Barbara Mathias); *Call of the Ages* by Tom Petrisko; *Messages and Teachings of Mary at Medjugorje* by Faith Publishing Company. Material dealing with Occult and New Age growth was taken from *The Power of the Occult*, by Terry Ann Modica (Faith Publishing Co.).

Additional material involving simple quotations or confirmations of facts, items of question or doubt, or short referrals to other articles or publications are not listed separately here.

Items identifying the position of the Church as to private revelation, used in this chapter, have been referenced in the previous three chapters.

NOTES: CHAPTER V

Much of the information regarding the development of the use of the Rosary and scapular, as well as detail on miracles associated with the use of the Rosary is contained in a small book, *The Power of the Rosary*, authored by Fr. Albert Shamon and published by The Riehle Foundation. Laurie Balbach-Taylor's profile on Pople John Paul II was taken from the book, *Priest of the World's Destiny*, published by Faith Publishing Company.

Pope John Paul II and his address concerning the Marian Movement and the importance of "centers of Marian piety" was featured in the January 28, 1996 edition of *Mary's People* newspaper. Additional material reflecting the positive aspects of the Marian Movement were taken from the book, *Thoughts*, and the audio cassettes of the talk, *Discernment*, both by the author of this book.

The book, *In Testimony*, is available from The Riehle Foundation. Additional segments detailing the growth of aspects of the Marian Movement during this century were taken from the works of John Haffert, from *Soul Magazine*, and from the history of the *Legion of Mary*, all referenced previously. Additional reference material was taken from the books listed in the above "Notes" for Chapters I, II, and III.

The Marian Movement of Priests organization, in this country (USA) is headquartered at P.O. Box 8, St. Francis, Maine, 04774. The organization publishes a book, with updates, of the messages and talks of Fr. Gobbi under the title of, *To the Priests, Our Lady's Beloved Sons*.

NOTES: CHAPTER VI AND VII

Reference to any other materials in these two chapters pertain to sources already noted in the first five chapters.

NOTES: APPENDIX

The guidelines and rules for discernment shown in the appendix segments were taken from the book, *Thoughts*, by this author; *Graces of Interior Prayer*, by Fr. A. Poulain; *The Three Ages of the Interior Life*, by Fr. R. Garrigou-LaGrange, and the *Spiritual Exercises of St. Ignatius Loyola*.

Material referring to specific apparition sites and/or visionaries was compiled from books, newsletters, tapes and correspondence from the organizations involved including: "Our Lady of Light Foundation," and "The Shepherds of Christ Ministries," regarding events in Ohio and Northern Kentucky; the *"Call to Peace"* publication in Arkansas; and the "Cross of Peace" apostolate in California. Additional information and confirmations thereto were taken from materials received by the author, from various sources and from any of the previous sources identified previously in this "notes" section.

THE RIEHLE FOUNDATION . . .

The Riehle Foundation is a non-profit, tax-exempt, charitable organization that exists to produce and/or distribute Catholic material to anyone, anywhere.

The Foundation is dedicated to the Mother of God and her role in the salvation of mankind. We believe that this role has not diminished in our time, but on the contrary has become all the more apparent in this the era of Mary as recognized by Pope John Paul II, whom we strongly support.

During the past five years the foundation has distributed over four million books, films, rosaries, bibles, etc. to individuals, parishes, and organizations all over the world. Additionally, the Foundation sends materials to missions and parishes in a dozen foreign countries.

Donations forwarded to The Riehle Foundation for the materials distributed provide our sole support. We appreciate your assistance, and request your prayers.

For copies of this book, or for a catalog of current titles, contact:

The Riehle Foundation
P.O. Box 7
Milford, OH 45150
513-576-0032